CRASH COURSE
FOR THE SAT
The Last-Minute Guide to
Scoring High

Fourth Edition

by Jeff Rubenstein

Random House, Inc.
New York

The Princeton Review, Inc.
111 Speen Street, Suite 550
Framingham, MA 01701
E-mail: editorialsupport@review.com

Published in the United States by Random House, Inc., New York, and simultaneously in Canada by Random House of Canada Limited, Toronto.

ISBN 978-0-375-42831-9
ISSN 1525-7177

Editor: Laura Braswell
Production Editor: Michael Mazzei
Production Coordinator: Deborah A. Silvestrini
Updated by: Eric Ginsberg

Printed in the United States of America on partially recycled paper.

9   8   7   6   5   4   3   2   1

Fourth Edition

ACKNOWLEDGMENTS

Many thanks to Eric Ginsberg for revising this edition. Thanks to Faisel Alam, Karen Lurie, Andy Lutz, and Rachel Warren for help and amusement.

Additional thanks to Christine Parker, Doug Pierce, and the Diagpalooza team.

Special thanks to Adam Robinson, who conceived of and perfected the Joe Bloggs approach to standardized tests, and many other techniques in this book.

ACKNOWLEDGMENTS

CONTENTS

INTRODUCTION

WHAT IS THE SAT?

Worried about the SAT? Have your friends, family, teachers, and pets been driving you crazy with conflicting information about the test? Not sure what to expect on test day? Well, relax, because The Princeton Review is here to help!

This book that you now hold in your hands will help you get acquainted with the SAT and improve your score on the test, all in ten simple steps. We'll tell you everything you need to know about the content and format of the SAT and show you our proven strategies for increasing your score. After working through our ten-step crash course, you'll be a more confident and more prepared test taker. Sound good? Okay, let's get started!

The SAT is a three-hour-and-45-minute standardized test used by many colleges as a factor in undergraduate admissions and placement decisions. The SAT consists of Math, Critical Reading, and Writing sections.

There are three scored Math sections with a total of 54 questions. Two of the Math sections are 25 minutes each; the third is 20 minutes. The math questions appear in two different formats: multiple-choice problem-solving questions and grid-ins.

The three scored Critical Reading sections contain a total of 67 questions. Two of the Critical Reading sections are 25 minutes each; the third is 20 minutes. All three Critical Reading sections begin with sentence completion. The two 25-minute sections contain short and long reading comprehension as well, while the 20-minute section contains only long reading comprehension.

Additionally, the SAT includes three scored Writing sections that test grammar and writing. The first is a 25-minute essay, and the second and third are 25- and 10-minute multiple-choice grammar sections with 54 questions in total. The types of grammar questions appearing on the test include error identifications, improving sentences, and improving paragraphs.

But wait, there's more. The SAT also has an unscored, experimental section that is always 25 minutes, and could be a Math, Critical Reading, or Writing section. This section is used to test questions for future administrations. Unfortunately, there is no reliable way to know which of the sections is experimental, so you'll have to do your best on all of them.

How Important Is the SAT?

Unfortunately, your SAT score is often one of the most important pieces of your admissions portfolio. If your scores fall below a school's usual range, the admissions officers may look very critically at the other parts of your application; if your scores exceed the school's usual range, you will have a leg up on many others in the applicant pool. In general, smaller and more selective schools tend to place more weight on other factors, such as your interview, your essays, and your extra-curricular activities. On the other hand, larger schools (which have a very large applicant pool to choose from) tend to rely more heavily on SAT scores and high school grade point average. At these schools, admissions decisions may be based entirely (or almost entirely) on these two factors. This is not true, however, of every school; some schools have begun to de-emphasize the SAT, and a few have even made it optional.

WHAT IS THE PSAT?

The PSAT is a test that's very similar to the SAT. (In fact, the PSAT is usually composed of previously administered SAT questions.) It is given by most high schools to students in their junior (and occasionally sophomore) year. The PSAT is used to help select National Merit Scholars, but unless you're one of the very few who are in contention for these scholarships, it's really only a practice test. Colleges will not see your PSAT scores; only your high school will. But if you're interested in doing well on the PSAT, all the techniques that you will learn in this book apply just as well to the PSAT as they do to the SAT.

WHO WRITES THIS TEST, ANYWAY?
WHAT WILL BE ON IT?

The SAT is written and administered by Educational Testing Service (ETS), under contract from the College Board. The people who work at ETS are average folks who just happen to make a living writing tests. They aren't paid to care about students; they're paid to write and administer tests.

The Math sections of the SAT test mostly basic arithmetic, algebra, and geometry. Only about 10 percent of the questions deal with more advanced concepts such as functions, manipulations with exponents, and properties of tangent lines. However, even if you're a math expert, there's no guarantee you'll do well on the test. The questions on the test are often confusingly worded, and ETS has planted plenty of trap choices to seduce you into picking incorrect answers. You may get the feeling at times that ETS has rigged the game against you—and you'd be right to feel that way. This book will review the math that you need to know, show you easier ways to solve the problems, and help you avoid ETS's traps.

The Critical Reading sections of the SAT test vocabulary and your ability to pick out facts from a reading passage. In this book, we'll help you improve your vocabulary and make the most of the vocabulary you already have. Moreover, we'll show you how to find facts in a passage efficiently with a technique that we've designed for the SAT.

The Writing sections of the SAT test your knowledge of a few simple rules of grammar as well as your ability to write a coherent essay in a short period of time. This book will review the rules of grammar that you need to know and show you some helpful tips on how to write the type of essay that ETS wants to see.

WHAT IS THE PRINCETON REVIEW?

The Princeton Review is the leader in test prep. Our goal is to help students everywhere crack the SAT. Ideally, we'd like the SAT to be eliminated altogether; we think the test is that bad. But until that happens, we'll content ourselves with aiding as many students as possible.

Starting from humble beginnings in 1981, The Princeton Review is now the nation's largest SAT preparation company. We offer courses in more than 500 locations in 12 different countries, as well as online; we also publish best-selling books, like the one you're holding, and software to get students ready for this test.

Our techniques work. We developed them after spending countless hours scrutinizing real SATs, analyzing them with computers, and proving our theories in the classroom. Our methods have been widely imitated, but no one achieves our score improvement.

How to Use This Book

This book is divided into two parts. The first part covers the basic concepts and techniques you need to know to improve your score. It is divided into ten steps, each of which should take about an hour to cover. Each step will introduce some new material and present some "Your Turn" drills to reinforce that material. Because vocabulary is so important to the Critical Reading section of the SAT, each step also includes a portion of The Princeton Review Hit Parade (the list of words that appear most frequently on the test).

The second part of the book is composed of some practice drills on which you can try out your newly acquired techniques. We suggest that you learn one step per day: read the technique chapters very carefully, do all of the "Your Turn" exercises, and learn the vocabulary for each step. If you still have time, try your hand at a few of the drills in the back of the book.

Because this book is a "crash course," it is intended to help you get the maximum improvement in a minimum amount of time. We won't waste your time going through every possible problem that might appear on the test. Rather, we'll teach you the essentials. If you have more time before the test, we highly recommend that you purchase *11 Practice Tests for the SAT & PSAT* (published by Random House), which will allow you to take practice SATs under timed conditions.

TEN STEPS

In the first two Steps, we'll discuss some general strategies to help you get the best possible score on the SAT, and introduce some techniques that you can use on every part of the test. Some of our advice may sound a bit strange at first. You may even find yourself saying, "But my teacher would kill me if I did this on a test in school!" Just remember: This isn't school. Our techniques are specifically designed to get you points on the SAT—and they work.

STEP 1

DO THE RIGHT NUMBER
OF PROBLEMS

Most students think they need to do every problem on the SAT to get great scores, and they hurt their scores because they try to do too many problems.

There are two reasons why it doesn't make sense to try every problem on the test. First, it's very hard to finish every question while maintaining a high level of accuracy. During timed tests, people naturally rush—and they make careless errors and lose points. Almost everyone is better off slowing down, using the whole time allowed to work on fewer problems, and answering more of those problems correctly.

You'll get a higher score if you do only 75 percent of the problems on this test and answer them correctly than if you do all of the problems and answer about half correctly. Likewise, you'll get a much higher score if you do only 50 percent of the problems on this test and answer them correctly than if you do three-quarters of them and only answer half correctly.

Here's how accuracy can help you: Let's say you answered every critical reading question on the test (65 questions). If you answered 33 correctly and 32 incorrectly, roughly translated, you would earn 33 raw points for the correct answers. But then you need to subtract your "penalty" for the incorrect answers. For every incorrect answer, ETS subtracts one-quarter of a point from your raw score. In this example, that would work out to 8 points. So instead of earning 33 points, you'd earn only 25 points (roughly a 470).

So, how do you crack it? Let's say you slowed down, answered only 45 questions, and left 20 questions blank—almost one-third of the test—ending up with 37 correct answers and eight incorrect answers. You'd earn 37 raw points for your correct answers and lose two points for the incorrect ones. So overall you'd earn 35 raw points (which is roughly a 550). In this example, you left 20 questions blank but ended up with a higher score! So remember, you can hurt yourself by answering every question.

Not every question is of the same level of difficulty; in fact, most of the problems on this test are arranged in increasing order of difficulty within their sections: The earlier questions are easier, and they get gradually harder until the final questions are so difficult that only a small percentage of test takers answers them correctly. A hard question is worth no more than an easy question, so why waste time working on it?

WHICH PROBLEMS SHOULD I DO?

You should do the problems that are easiest for you. In general, the questions on the SAT are arranged in increasing order of difficulty.

The first third of the questions in a section are easy questions. The next third of the questions are medium-difficulty questions, and the last third of the questions are hard. For example, on a 20-question problem-solving section, the first six to seven questions will be easy, the next six to seven will be medium, and the last six to seven will be hard. On the 20-question section that has both problem solving and grid-ins, the order of difficulty resets with the grid-in questions; that is, even though the first grid-in question is number 11, it is an easy question.

The most important question to ask yourself when you approach a problem on the SAT is: How difficult is it? If it's an easy question, go ahead and answer it. If it's a medium or hard question, be careful! Try to avoid solving these problems in the usual way. Instead, use one of our techniques, or try to take a good guess using Process of Elimination (POE), which you'll learn about in Step 2.

Learning to identify the easiest questions for you is *so* important that we've given all of the problems in this book the question number that they would have on an actual SAT. Remember to always ask yourself: Is this question easy, medium, or hard? Should I do this problem, and if so, how should I approach it?

HOW MANY PROBLEMS SHOULD I DO?

Only the number of problems you need. You're much better off doing fewer problems and increasing your accuracy than doing too many problems and getting too few of them right.

The following charts show you how many problems you need to answer correctly in order to get a certain score. You should use all the time you're given to do only the number of problems indicated by the charts, and answer them correctly. (The numbers in the charts allow for a small margin of error.)

Math

On the Math section, for instance, if you're aiming for a 550, you should do only 14 of the problems in the 20-question problem-solving section. Which 14 problems? The 14 that you like the best. Many of them will probably be among the first 14; but if you don't like problem number 13, skip it and do number 15 instead.

		Answer this many questions				
			18-Question section			
To get (scaled score)	You need to earn (raw points)	20-question section	8 Multiple choice	10 Grid-ins	16-question section	Total # of questions to attempt
350	7	6	2	2	2	12
400	12	7	3	3	4	17
450	19	9	4	4	6	23
500	25	11	5	5	8	29
550	32	14	6	6	10	36
600	38	16	6	7	13	42
650	44	18	7	8	15	48
700	47	all	all	9	all	53
750	52	all	all	all	all	54
800	54	all	all	all	all	54

Critical Reading

The next chart is for Critical Reading. If you're aiming for a 550, you need to answer a total of 38 problems correctly. Which 38? The ones that you like best. If you're strong in reading comprehension, maybe you'll try for 27 reading comprehension points and 11 sentence completions. If you're weak in reading comprehension, you'd aim for 17 sentence completions, and 19 reading comprehension questions. It's up to you. It's a good idea, though, to have a game plan in advance. Find one that plays to your strengths.

To get (scaled score)	You need to earn (raw points)	Answer this many questions			Total # of questions to attempt
		23- to 25-question section	23- to 25-question section	19-question section	
300	5	6	6	3	15
350	9	8	8	4	20
400	14	11	11	8	30
450	21	15	15	12	42
500	29	20	20	14	54
550	38	23	23	18	64
600	46	all	all	all	65–69
650	53	all	all	all	65–69
700	59	all	all	all	65–69
750	63	all	all	all	65–69
800	67	all	all	all	65–69

Essay & Grammar

Your Writing score will be computed by combining your essay score and your score from the multiple-choice grammar section. The grammar section, which accounts for roughly 70 percent of your total score, is scored the same way as are the other multiple-choice sections on the test—one point for a correct answer, zero points for a question left blank, and minus one-quarter point for a wrong answer. Your essay is scored on a two- to twelve-point scale; this score is then doubled. The final total from your essay is added to your grammar score to arrive at your Writing score.

Grammar Score (Raw Points)	Essay Score						
	12	10	8	6	4	2	0
80 (49)	800	800	790	750	720	690	680
75 (47)	800	770	730	690	670	640	620
70 (44)	750	710	670	640	610	580	570
65 (41)	710	680	640	600	580	550	530
60 (37)	670	640	600	560	540	510	490
55 (32)	630	590	550	520	490	460	450
50 (27)	590	560	520	480	460	430	410
45 (20)	540	510	470	430	410	380	360
40 (15)	500	470	430	400	370	340	330
35 (9)	460	430	390	350	330	300	280
30 (5)	420	390	350	320	290	260	250
25 (1)	370	340	300	270	240	210	200
20 (-2)	320	290	250	210	200	200	200

For example, let's say you answered 36 multiple-choice questions correctly and eight incorrectly and received an essay score of eight. You would earn 34 points from the multiple-choice sections and 16 points from the essay (remember to double the essay score) for a total of 50 points.

While this seems like quite a bit of math for a Writing section, the important thing to keep in mind is the impact your essay can have on your Writing score. A good essay can really boost your score; similarly, a poor essay will hurt your score.

SET REASONABLE GOALS

If you're currently scoring 500, trying to score a 650 right away will only hurt you. Try to work your way up in easy stages. Pick a score range approximately 50 points higher than the range in which you're currently scoring. If you're currently scoring 500, aim for a 550; when you have reached 550, then you can aim for 600.

If you haven't ever taken a practice SAT, you can estimate your current SAT score by looking at your PSAT score. Add a zero to your PSAT score to see roughly what you would score on the SAT. For instance, if you scored a 50 Critical Reading and 55 Math on the PSAT, that corresponds to a 500 Critical Reading and 550 Math on the SAT.

SLOW DOWN.

Do fewer problems.

Answer more problems correctly.

Do the problems that are easiest for you.

Vocab Time

Turn to page 149 and memorize the Hit Parade Words for Step 1.

STEP 2

LEARN TO USE PROCESS OF ELIMINATION

GUESS AGGRESSIVELY

Guessing aggressively basically means that if you can eliminate even one answer choice on a problem, you should take a guess.

You may have heard from various sources that the SAT has a guessing penalty, and that you shouldn't guess on the SAT. This is false. You should guess aggressively and often on the SAT. Here's why: To generate your final score, ETS first computes your raw score. ETS gives you one raw score point for every correct answer and subtracts one-quarter of a raw score point for every wrong answer on your bubble sheet. Blanks are not counted at all. This raw score is then converted to a scaled score on the 200–800 scale.

The SAT (or most of it, anyway) is a five-option, multiple-choice test. If you guess completely randomly on five questions in a row, you should—by random chance—get one of these five correct and four of them wrong. Because you'd get one point for the one correct answer, and lose a quarter of a point for each of the four wrong answers, your net raw score would be zero.

HINT
Random guessing will not help or hurt you on the SAT. It simply counts for nothing.

So while it is true that you lose a fraction of a point for every incorrect answer on the test, this only has the effect of neutralizing completely random guessing. Guessing randomly has no effect on your score at all.

This means that you shouldn't waste your time by randomly guessing. However—and this is why you should guess aggressively and often—if you can eliminate even one choice and guess better than randomly, then guessing will increase your score. So you should get in the habit of guessing aggressively. Even if you can't get the correct answer, you should eliminate the choices you know are impossible or unreasonable, guess from the choices that remain, and move on to the next problem.

You don't have to know how to solve a problem in order to get the correct answer (or at least to be able to make a good guess). Aggressively using **Process of Elimination** (which we'll call **POE** from now on) will get you points on the SAT.

    1.   What is the capital of Malawi?

If you were to see this problem on the SAT (don't worry, you won't), you'd probably be stuck—not to mention a little upset. But the majority of the problems on the SAT don't look like the problem above. They look like the following:

    1.   What is the capital of Malawi?
       (A) Washington
       (B) Paris
       (C) Tokyo
       (D) London
       (E) Lilongwe

Not so bad anymore, is it? By knowing which choices must be wrong, you can often figure out what the answer is—even without knowing *why* it's the correct answer.

We will discuss POE for each problem type throughout the book, but there are two general principles of POE that you should learn right away: **Estimation** and **Joe Bloggs**.

ESTIMATION

On math problems, you may be able to use common sense and estimate an answer before trying to solve it. Often, several of the answers are unreasonable and can be eliminated right away. This will help you avoid careless mistakes and make good guesses, even if you can't solve the problems.

Read the following:

> **5.** If 12 cans of food can feed 8 dogs for one
>   week, how many cans of food would be
>   needed to feed 6 dogs for two weeks?
>
>   (A) 9
>   (B) 12
>   (C) 16
>   (D) 18
>   (E) 24

Before you start to calculate, estimate. If 12 cans will feed 8
dogs for one week, and you want to know how many cans are
needed for two weeks, the answer must be larger than 12. So
eliminate A and B. But six dogs are only being fed for two
weeks, so the answer must be less than 24. Eliminate E. The
answer must be either C or D. Now, if you can calculate the
answer, great. If not, you've got a 50 percent chance of a correct
guess.

You can estimate a lot more on the SAT than you might
think, particularly on geometry. Estimate whenever you can!

JOE BLOGGS

Suppose for a moment that you could look at the answers
recorded by the tester next to you (you can't). Also suppose
that you know for a fact that every one of your neighbor's
answers on the test is wrong. If, on problem 23, that person
marked C as his or her answer, what would you do? Eliminate
choice C, right?

Well, even though you can't look at your neighbor's page,
you can use this principle to get points on the test. We've created an imaginary tester to accompany you during the exam, a
tester that we've named Joe Bloggs.

Now, Joe isn't stupid, he's just average. And when ETS test
writers write the SAT, they write it in a very particular way.
They write it so that Joe will get most of the easy problems correct, some of the medium problems correct, and none of the
hard ones correct.

How do they do this? The test writers are very good at predicting what kinds of answer choices are attractive to the average person. They're good at it because they've been doing it for more than 40 years.

Joe Bloggs, the average test taker, always picks the answer that first attracts him. Choices that first attract him on math problems have nice round numbers that can be easily derived from other numbers in the problem. Choices that attract him on critical reading questions have familiar words that remind him of words in the question.

Question Type	Joe Bloggs Selects	How Joe Does
Easy	What Seems Right	Mostly Right
Medium	What Seems Right	So-So
Hard	What Seems Right	All Wrong!

What does this mean for you? When you're working on easy problems, pick the choice that seems right to you. When you're working on medium problems, be careful. If you got the answer too quickly, check your work. Medium problems should take more work than easy problems. If you're working on hard problems, eliminate the choices that first seem attractive; they are almost always traps.

Remember, though: Joe Bloggs gets the easy problems right. *Cross off Joe Bloggs answers only on the hard problems.* And don't forget: How do you know how hard a question is? By its question number.

Read the following example:

8. The manager rushed from the dugout and pulled his star player away from the umpire, fearing that the batter's impassioned protests would only _____ the situation and result in the player's ejection.

(A) compromise
(B) alleviate
(C) denigrate
(D) militate
(E) officiate

First, read the question number. This is sentence completion number 8 out of 8, which means it's a hard question. You may not know what militate or denigrate mean, but you (and Joe) probably know what some of the other words mean. Joe likes to pick words that are familiar and sound good in the sentence, so he'll probably go with choice A or B; therefore, because this is a hard question, you should eliminate Joe's choices. Even if you can't eliminate any others, take a guess from among C, D, and E. In fact, the answer is D.

Read this math problem:

20. Michelle rode her bicycle from her house to school at an average speed of 8 miles per hour. Later that day, she rode from school back home along the same route at an average speed of 12 miles per hour. If the round trip took her 1 hour, how many miles long is the round trip?

(A) 8
(B) $9\frac{3}{5}$
(C) 10
(D) $11\frac{1}{5}$
(E) 12

Which choice do you think seems attractive to Joe at first? Because he sees the numbers 8 and 12 and the word "average," he will probably average 8 and 12 to get 10. Therefore, Joe will pick C.

But now you know better. This problem is number 20, the hardest problem in the section. You know that Joe will get it wrong, so eliminate his choice, C.

If Joe doesn't pick C, what else might he pick? Either A, 8, or E, 12, because those are the numbers that appear in the problem. Cross them off as well. Then guess from either B or D. (The answer is B. But we're not going to spend time on why.) If you can quickly cross off a few choices on a hard problem and make a good guess, you'll be in great shape.

HINT

Use POE and Joe Bloggs. They are your best friends on the SAT.

Guess aggressively. If you can cross off even one answer choice, take a guess!

Vocab Time

Turn to pages 150–151 and memorize the Hit Parade Words for Step 2.

KNOW YOUR
DEFINITIONS—PART 1

The greatest number of errors on SAT Math actually occur in reading comprehension: Test takers misunderstand what the question is asking. Learn the following definitions well, and practice them on real problems.

THE BASICS PART I

Integers are numbers that have no fractional or decimal parts.
Examples of integers are –10, –3, –2, –1, 0, 1, 2, 3, 10, 23, and 50. What kinds of numbers are not integers? 2.3, $\frac{1}{2}$, .6666, and so on.

Positive numbers are numbers that are larger than zero. Zero is *not* positive. Examples of positive numbers are $\frac{1}{2}$, 1, 2.33, and 5.

Negative numbers are numbers that are less than zero. Zero is *not* negative. Examples of negative numbers are $-\frac{1}{2}$, –1, –2.33, and –5.

Even numbers are integers that can be divided by 2 with no remainder. Examples of even numbers are –4, –2, 0, 2, 4, and 6. Zero is even, even though it is neither positive nor negative!

Odd numbers are integers that cannot be divided evenly by 2. Examples of odd numbers are –3, –1, 1, 3, 5, and 7.

Factors are the integers by which an integer can be divided with no remainder. The easiest way to find them is in pairs. For instance, 12 can be written as 1×12, 2×6, or 3×4. 12 can be divided by 1, 2, 3, 4, 6, and 12. These numbers are the factors of 12.

Multiples are the integers that can be divided by an integer. The easiest way to find multiples is to count up, adding the same number each time. $12 \times 1 = 12$; $12 \times 2 = 24$; $12 \times 3 = 36$.... So, the first three positive multiples of 12 are 12, 24, and 36. But we can keep counting up by 12s forever: 12, 24, 36, 48, 60, 72, 84.... *All* of these numbers are multiples of 12.

> ### HINT
>
> If you tend to confuse factors and multiples, remember this tip: Factors are Few, Multiples are Many. There are only a few factors for any given number, but there is always an infinite number of multiples!

Prime numbers are numbers that can be divided only by 1 and themselves. The first six prime numbers are 2, 3, 5, 7, 11, and 13. Zero and 1 are not prime, and 2 is the only even prime.

Distinct numbers are different numbers. For example, how many distinct numbers are there in the set {2, 5, 2, 6, 5, 7}? There are only four distinct numbers in this set: 2, 5, 6, and 7.

A *digit* is a figure from 0 through 9 that holds a place. For instance, the number 345.862 is composed of six digits. The digit 3 is in the *hundreds* place, the digit 4 is in the *tens* place, and the digit 5 is in the *units* place. The digit 8 is in the *tenths* place, the digit 6 is in the *hundredths* place, and the digit 2 is in the *thousandths* place.

Your Turn—Exercise 3.1

    a. What are three consecutive odd integers whose sum is 15? _____

    b. What are the factors of 10? _____

    c. What are the prime factors of 10? _____

    d. What are the factors of 36? _____

    e. What are the prime factors of 36? _____

    f. What are the first seven positive multiples of 6? _____

g. What are the first seven positive multiples of 4? _____

h. Numbers that are multiples of both 6 and 5 are also multiples of _____.

1. Which of the following does NOT have a remainder of 1?

(A) $\dfrac{15}{7}$

(B) $\dfrac{17}{8}$

(C) $\dfrac{51}{3}$

(D) $\dfrac{61}{4}$

(E) $\dfrac{81}{10}$

2. Which of the following numbers has the digit 4 in the thousandths place?

(A) 4000.0
(B)   40.0
(C)   0.4
(D)   0.04
(E)   0.004

3. Which of the following numbers is NOT prime?

(A) 11
(B) 23
(C) 27
(D) 29
(E) 31

Answers to Exercise 3.1

a. 3, 5, 7

b. 1, 2, 5, 10

c. 2, 5

d. 1, 2, 3, 4, 6, 9, 12, 18, 36

e. 2, 3

f. 6, 12, 18, 24, 30, 36, 42

g. 4, 8, 12, 16, 20, 24, 28

h. 30

1. **C** 51 can be divided evenly by 3 with no remainder.

2. **E** The thousandths place is the third to the right of the decimal.

3. **C** 27 can be divided by 3 and 9.

THE BASICS PART II

Consecutive numbers are numbers that are "in a row." 4, 5, and 6 are consecutive integers; 6, 8, and 10 are consecutive *even* integers.

Divisible means divisible with no remainder. 6 is divisible by 3, but 6 is not divisible by 5.

The *remainder* is what is left over after you divide. For example, when you divide 18 by 8, there is a remainder of 2.

A *sum* is the result of addition.

A *difference* is the result of subtraction.

A *product* is the result of multiplication.

A *quotient* is the result of division.

Your Turn—Exercise 3.2

a. The product of two positive integers x and y is 30 and their sum is 11. What are x and y? _____

b. The product of two positive integers x and y is 30 and their difference is 13. What are x and y? _____

4. What is the least of three consecutive integers whose sum is 21?

(A) 4
(B) 5
(C) 6
(D) 7
(E) 8

5. If a, b, c, d, and e are consecutive even integers, and $a < b < c < d < e$, then $d + e$ is how much greater than $a + b$?

(A) 10
(B) 12
(C) 14
(D) 16
(E) 18

6. All numbers divisible by both 3 and 14 are also divisible by which of the following?

(A) 6
(B) 9
(C) 16
(D) 28
(E) 32

Answers to Exercise 3.2

a. 5 and 6

b. 15 and 2

4. **C**   The three consecutive integers must be 6, 7, and 8. The least of them is 6.

5. **B**   If the numbers are 2, 4, 6, 8, and 10, then $8 + 10 = 18$ and $2 + 4 = 6$. The last two numbers are 12 greater than the first two. (Don't forget that the numbers have to be consecutive and even!)

6. **A**   Look at the numbers that can be divided by 3 and 14. What is the first such number? 42. The only number in the answer choices that divides evenly into 42 is 6.

ADVANCED ARITHMETIC—EXPONENTS AND SQUARE ROOTS

Exponents are easy to deal with, if you write them out. $3^3 = 3 \times 3 \times 3$. You can multiply and divide exponents that have the same base.

When you multiply, add the exponents:
$$3^4 \times 3^3 = 3 \times 3 \times 3 \times 3 \times 3 \times 3 \times 3 = 3^7$$

When you divide them, subtract the exponents.
$$\frac{3^4}{3^3} = \frac{3 \times 3 \times 3 \times 3}{3 \times 3 \times 3} = 3^1$$

If you raise an exponent to a power, multiply the exponents.
$$(3^2)^3 = 3 \times 3 \times 3 \times 3 \times 3 \times 3 = 3^6$$

Two special rules:
- Anything to the zero power is equal to 1: $3^0 = 1$

- Anything to the first power is equal to itself: $3^1 = 3$

When you solve a rational exponent, such as $4^{\frac{3}{2}}$, first raise 4 to the 3rd power: $4 \times 4 \times 4 = 64$. Then, take the square root, or second square root, of this number: $\sqrt{64} = 8$. So, $4^{\frac{3}{2}} = 8$. The numerator is your exponent and the denominator is your radical.

*Finding a **square root*** is just the opposite of raising a number to the second power. $\sqrt{4} = 2$, because $2^2 = 4$.

Square roots work just like exponents: You can *always* multiply and divide roots, but you can only add and subtract with the *same* root.

Multiplication and Division:

- $\sqrt{8} \times \sqrt{2} = \sqrt{16} = 4$
- $\sqrt{\dfrac{1}{4}} = \dfrac{\sqrt{1}}{\sqrt{4}} = \dfrac{1}{2}$
- $\sqrt{400} = \sqrt{4 \times 100} = \sqrt{4} \times \sqrt{100} = 2 \times 10 = 20$

Addition and Subtraction:

- $2\sqrt{2} + 3\sqrt{2} = 5\sqrt{2}$
- $4\sqrt{3} - \sqrt{3} = 3\sqrt{3}$
- $2\sqrt{3} + 3\sqrt{2}$ *cannot be added easily, because the terms do not have the same root.*

Your Turn—Exercise 3.3

    a. $3^3 \times 3^2 = $ _____

    b. $\dfrac{3^3}{3^2} = $ _____

    c. $(3^3)^2 = $ _____

    d. $x^6 \times x^2 = $ _____

    e. $\dfrac{x^6}{x^2} = $ _____

    f. $(x^6)^2 = $ _____

    g. $9^{\frac{2}{4}} = $ _____

    3. If $3^4 = 9^x$, then $x = $

        (A) 2

        (B) 3

        (C) 4

        (D) 5

        (E) 6

5. If $(3^x)^3 = 3^{15}$, what is the value of x ?

(A) 3

(B) 5

(C) 7

(D) 9

(E) 12

10. If $x^y \times x^6 = x^{54}$ and $(x^3)^z = x^9$, then
$y + z =$

(A) 10

(B) 11

(C) 48

(D) 50

(E) 51

Answers to Exercise 3.3

a. 3^5

b. 3^1

c. 3^6

d. x^8

e. x^4

f. x^{12}

g. 3

3. **A**   If $3^4 = 9^x$, then $81 = 9^x$. Therefore, $x = 2$. You could also rewrite 3^4 as $3 \times 3 \times 3 \times 3 = 9 \times 9$.

5. **B**   If $(3^x)^3 = 3^{15}$, and you know that $x \times 3 = 15$, then $x = 5$.

10. **E**   Because $x^y \times x^6 = x^{54}$, y must be 48. Likewise, because $(x^3)^z = x^9$, z must be 3. Therefore, $y + z = 51$.

EASY ALGEBRA—SIMULTANEOUS EQUATIONS

Simultaneous equations are usually cumbersome, lengthy problems that require you to solve for one variable in terms of the other and then plug that into the other equation and solve for one of the variables. Confused? Well, don't be—on the SAT, simultaneous equations are easy! Just **Stack and Combine** the equations.

1. If $2x - 3y = 7$ and $3x - 2y = 24$, what does $5x - 5y = ?$

Here's How to Crack It

Don't try to solve for x or y individually—instead write them like this:

$$2x - 3y = 7$$
$$\underline{+\ 3x - 2y = 24}$$

Now if you add the equations, the problem becomes very simple!

$$2x - 3y = 7$$
$$\underline{+\ 3x - 2y = 24}$$
$$5x - 5y = 31$$

So remember, if you have simultaneous equations, Stack and Combine. Sometimes you'll have to add the equations, and other times, you'll simply subtract one from the other. If you're not sure what to do, then add them—if it works, great; if not, then try subtracting.

Now try this one:

2. If $6x - 7y = 13$ and $5x - 8y = -13$, what does $2x + 2y = ?$

Here's How to Crack It

Again, if you try and solve for x or y, then you'll spend too much time doing this equation more than once. So stack 'em!

$$\begin{array}{r} 6x - 7y = 13 \\ - \underline{5x - 8y = -13} \\ x + y = 26 \end{array}$$

At this point, you have $x + y$, but you need $2x + 2y$. So multiply both sides by two!

$$2(x + y) = 2(26)$$

Therefore:

$$2x + 2y = 52$$

Vocab Time

Turn to pages 151–152 and memorize the Hit Parade Words for Step 3.

STEP 4

KNOW YOUR DEFINITIONS—PART 2

AVERAGE, PERCENT, AND PERCENT CHANGE

Average (arithmetic mean) = $\dfrac{\text{total}}{\text{\# of things}}$. If you know any two

of these parts, you can always solve for the third. If a student's

test scores are 60, 65, and 75, the average score for those tests =

$\dfrac{60+65+75}{3} = 66.67$. If a student had an average score of 50 on

three tests, the total score can be calculated, because the aver-

age (50) = $\dfrac{\text{total}}{3}$. Therefore his total score must have been 150.

Percent just means "divided by 100." So $20\% = \dfrac{20}{100} = \dfrac{1}{5} = 0.2$.

Likewise, $8\% = \dfrac{8}{100} = \dfrac{2}{25} = 0.08$.

Any percent question can be translated into algebra—just use the following rules!

Word	Translates to
Percent	100
Of	×
What	x (or any variable)
Is, Are, Equals	=

8 percent of 10 is	*becomes*	$0.08 \times 10 = 0.8$
10 percent of 80 is	*becomes*	$0.1 \times 80 = 8$
5 is what percent of 80?	*becomes*	$5 = \dfrac{x}{100} \times 80$
5 is 80 percent of what number?	*becomes*	$5 = \dfrac{80}{100} x$
What percent of 5 is 80?	*becomes*	$\dfrac{x}{100} \times 5 = 80$

Percent increase or percent decrease is always $\dfrac{\text{change}}{\text{original amount}}$.

If an \$80 item is reduced to \$60 during a sale, the percent decrease is the change in price (\$20) over the original amount (\$80), or 25%.

> ### HINT
>
> If the question asks for the percent increase, then the original is the *smaller* number. Conversely, if the question is asking for percent decrease, then the original will be the *bigger* number.

Your Turn—Exercise 4.1

a. If a student scores 70, 90, 95, and 105 on four tests, what is the average test score?

_____

b. If a student has an average score of 80 on four tests, what is the total of the scores received on those tests? _____

c. If a student has an average of 60 on tests whose totals add up to 360, how many tests has the student taken? _____

d. If the average of 4 and x is equal to the average of 2, 8, and x, what is the value of x ?

_____

e. The average (arithmetic mean) of 4 numbers is 80. If two of the numbers are 50 and 60, what is the sum of the other two numbers?

_____

f. What percent of 5 is 6? _____

g. 60 percent of 90 is the same as 50 percent of what number? _____

14. A group of 30 adults and 20 children went to the beach. If 50 percent of the adults and 80 percent of the children went swimming, what percent of the group went swimming?

(A) 30%

(B) 46%

(C) 50%

(D) 62%

(E) 65%

h. Jenny's salary increased from $30,000 to $33,000. By what percent did her salary increase? _____

i. In 1980, factory X produced 18,600 pieces. In 1981, factory X only produced 16,000 pieces. By approximately what percent did production decrease from 1980 to 1981? _____

j. Jennifer took 6 tests and had an average score of 76 on those tests. If she takes two additional tests and receives a final average of 80 for all of her tests, what was her average on the two additional tests?

_____

Answers to Exercise 4.1

a. 90

b. 320

c. 6

d. $x = 8$

e. 210

f. 120%

g. 108

14. **D**   50% of the adults = 15, and 80% of the children = 16,
    so 31 people total went swimming. 31 out of 50 is 62%.

h. 10%

i. $\dfrac{2,600}{18,600}$ = approximately 14% decrease.

j. 92

GEOMETRY DEFINITIONS

The *area* **of a square** or **rectangle** is *length × width*.

The *area* **of a parallelogram** is *base × height*.

The *area* **of a triangle** is $\frac{1}{2}$ *base × height*.

The *area* **of a circle** with radius r is πr^2, so a circle with a radius
of 5 has an area of 25π.

The *perimeter* of any object is the sum of the lengths of its
sides. A triangle with sides 3, 4, and 5 has a perimeter of 12.

The *circumference* of a circle with radius r is $2\pi r$, so a circle
with a radius of 5 has a circumference of 10π.

The **equation of a line** is written in the following form:
$y = mx + b$ in which y is the y-coordinate, m is the slope of
the line, x is the x-coordinate, and b is the y-intercept; i.e.,
the point where the line crosses the y-axis (the point at
which $x = 0$).

The *slope* of a line is equal to $\dfrac{rise}{run}$. To find the slope, first take any two points on the line and count off the perpendicular distance you need to get from one of these points to the other, as follows:

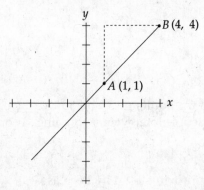

In the graph above, to get from point *A* to point *B*, we count up (rise) 3 points, and over (run) 3 points. So the slope is

$$\frac{\text{rise}}{\text{run}} = \frac{3}{3} = 1$$

No figure? No problem! If you need to find slope remember it's **rise** (the change in y-coordinates) over the **run** (the change in x-coordinates).

As a formula, slope $= \dfrac{(y_2 - y_1)}{(x_2 - x_1)}$.

Your Turn—Exercise 4.2

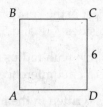

a. What is the area of square *ABCD* above?

_____

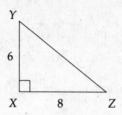

b. What is the area of triangle *XYZ* above?

_____

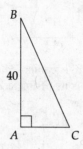

c. If the area of triangle *ABC* is 400, what is its base?_____

d. What is the area of the circle above with center *O* ?_____

e. What is its circumference? _____

f. If *ABCD* is a rectangle, *x* = _____, and
    y = _____.

g. What is the perimeter of rectangle *ABCD* ?

h. If the above figure is composed of two
    rectangles, what is its perimeter?

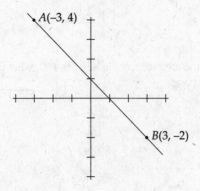

i. How many points do you count up (rise)
    to get from point *B* to point *A* ?

j. How many points must you count over
    (run) to get from point *B* to point *A* ?

k. What is the slope of the line above?

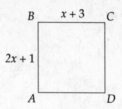

5. If *ABCD* is a square, what is its area?

   (A) 2
   (B) 3
   (C) 5
   (D) 20
   (E) 25

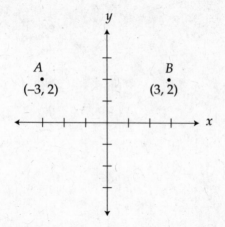

10. Which of the following is a point that is NOT
    on line $\overleftrightarrow{AB}$ (not shown)?

    (A) (−3, 2)
    (B) (0, 2)
    (C) (1, 2)
    (D) (3, 2)
    (E) (2, 3)

Answers to Exercise 4.2

a. 36

b. 24

c. 20

d. 9π

e. 6π

f. 10, 5

g. 30

h. 22

i. 6

j. −6

k. −1

5. **E**

10. **E**

WHAT'S A GRID-IN?

You will see ten questions on the SAT that ask you to bubble in a numerical answer on a grid rather than answer a multiple-choice question—these are **grid-in questions**.

Grid-ins are arranged in order of difficulty, and can be solved according to the methods already described for the multiple-choice problems on the test.

The only problem you might have with grid-ins is getting used to the way in which you are asked to answer the questions. For each question, you'll have a grid like the following:

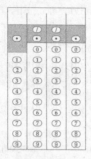

We recommend that you write the answer on top of the grid to help you bubble, but it's important to know that the scoring machine only reads the bubbles.

HINT

If you bubble incorrectly, the computer will mark the answer wrong.

THE BASIC RULES OF GRIDDING

If your answer (which will be a number) uses fewer than 4 boxes, you can grid it anywhere you like; you can grid an answer that needs 3 spaces in any of the 4 boxes, but to avoid confusion, we suggest that you start at the leftmost box.

You can grid your answer as either a fraction or a decimal if the fraction will fit.

You can grid an answer of .5 as either .5 or $\left[\frac{1}{2}\right]$.

You do not need to reduce your fractions if the fraction will fit.

If your answer is $\frac{2}{4}$, you can grid it as $\left[\frac{2}{4}\right]$, $\left[\frac{1}{2}\right]$, or .5.

If you have a decimal that will not fit in the spaces provided, you must grid as many places as will fit.

If your answer is $\frac{1}{3}$, you can grid it as $\left[\frac{1}{3}\right]$ or .333, but .33 is not acceptable.

You do not need to round your numbers, so we suggest that you don't.

You cannot grid mixed numbers. Convert all mixed numbers to ordinary fractions.

If your answer is $2\frac{1}{2}$, you must convert it to $\left[\frac{5}{2}\right]$ or 2.5.

Try the Following Grid-Ins:

a. 125   **b.** $\dfrac{2}{12}$ **c.** $3\dfrac{1}{4}$ **d.** .8958

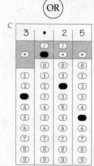

Answers to Grid-Ins

Your Turn—Exercise 4.3

17. On the first four flights out of LaGuardia this morning, there were 120, 110, 85, and 90 passengers. What was the median number of passengers?

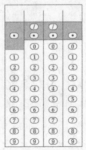

19. The sum of five consecutive integers, arranged in order from least to greatest, is 100. What is the sum of the next four consecutive integers?

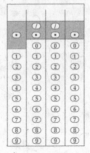

20. If $5x^2 = 125$, what is the value of $5x^3$?

	/	/	
.	.	.	.
	0	0	0
1	1	1	1
2	2	2	2
3	3	3	3
4	4	4	4
5	5	5	5
6	6	6	6
7	7	7	7
8	8	8	8
9	9	9	9

22. If 40 percent of 200 is equal to 300 percent of n, then n is equal to what number?

	/	/	
.	.	.	.
	0	0	0
1	1	1	1
2	2	2	2
3	3	3	3
4	4	4	4
5	5	5	5
6	6	6	6
7	7	7	7
8	8	8	8
9	9	9	9

Answers to Exercise 4.3

17. Since there were an even number of flights, to find the median, arrange the number of passengers from least to greatest. Then take the two middle numbers (90 and 110) and divide by 2.

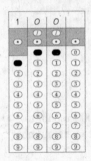

19. If five consecutive integers have a sum of 100, they must be 18, 19, 20, 21, and 22. The next four consecutive integers are 23, 24, 25, and 26. Their sum is 98.

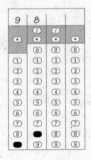

20. Because $5x^2 = 125$, we know that $x^2 = 25$ and $x = 5$. Therefore, $5x^3 = 5 \times 125 = 625$.

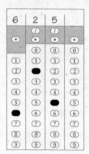

22. 40 percent of 200 is equal to $\frac{40}{100} \times 200 = 80$. So 80 is 300 percent of n. We can solve for n by translating this as $80 = \frac{300}{100} \times n$. So n must be $\frac{80}{3}$ or 26.667 (which you could grid either as 26.6 or 26.7).

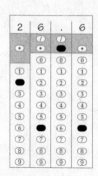

Vocab Time

Turn to pages 152–153 and memorize the Hit Parade Words for Step 4.

STEP 5

PLUGGING IN

PLUGGING IN YOUR OWN NUMBERS

The problem with doing algebra is that it's very easy to make mistakes. Whenever you see a problem with variables in the answer choices, Plug In. Start by picking a number for the variable in the problem (or for more than one variable, if necessary), solve the problem using that real number, and then see which answer choice gives you the correct answer.

Read the following problem:

2. If x is a positive integer, then 20 percent of $5x$ equals

    (A) x
    (B) $2x$
    (C) $5x$
    (D) $15x$
    (E) $20x$

Start by picking a number for x. Plug In a round number like 10. When you Plug In 10 for x, change every x in the problem into a 10. Now the problem reads:

2. If 10 is a positive integer, then 20 percent of 5(10) equals

    (A) 10
    (B)   2(10)
    (C)   5(10)
    (D) 15(10)
    (E) 20(10)

Look how easy the problem becomes! Now you can solve: 20 percent of 50 is 10. Which answer is 10? A.

Try it again:

8. If $-1 < x < 0$, then which of the following
    has the greatest value?

    (A) x

    (B) x^2

    (C) x^3

    (D) $\dfrac{1}{x}$

    (E) $2x$

This time when you pick a number for x, you have to make sure that it is between -1 and 0, because that's what the problem dictates. So try $-\dfrac{1}{2}$. If we make every x in the problem $-\dfrac{1}{2}$, the problem now reads:

8. If $-1 < -\dfrac{1}{2} < 0$, then which of the
    following has the greatest value?

    (A) $-\dfrac{1}{2}$

    (B) $\left(-\dfrac{1}{2}\right)^2 = \dfrac{1}{4}$

    (C) $\left(-\dfrac{1}{2}\right)^3 = -\dfrac{1}{8}$

    (D) $-\dfrac{1}{\frac{1}{2}} = -2$

    (E) $2\left(-\dfrac{1}{2}\right) = -1$

Now you can solve the problem. Which has the greatest value? Choice A is $-\frac{1}{2}$, choice B equals $\frac{1}{4}$, choice C equals $-\frac{1}{8}$, choice D equals -2, and choice E equals -1. So choice B is the greatest.

Plugging In is such a great technique that it makes even the hardest algebra problems easy. Anytime you can, Plug In!

Try one more:

> **9.** The average of four consecutive multiples of 3 is a.
> What is the value of the largest of the numbers?
> (A) $a + 6$
> (B) $a + 4.5$
> (C) $a + 3$
> (D) $a + 1.5$
> (E) a

Here's How to Crack It

Are there variables in the answer choices? Absolutely, so Plug In! Pick 4 consecutive multiples of 3: for example, 3, 6, 9, and 12. What's the average of your multiples? Well, $3 + 6 + 9 + 12 = 30$. Divide that result by 4 and we have 7.5, which is our a. The question asks for the *largest* of the numbers, which, for the above example, is 12—circle it! This is your *target* value. Now, simply Plug In a and see which answer works.

(A) $7.5 + 6 = 13.5$ not 12, so cross it off!
(B) $7.5 + 4.5 = 12$ BINGO! But check the other answers, too!
(C) $7.5 + 3 = 10.5$ not 12, so cross it off!
(D) $7.5 + 1.5 = 9$ not 12, so cross it off!
(E) 7.5 not 12, so cross it off!

Easy, huh? Of course, because you made the algebra into simple arithmetic!

What If There's No Variable?

Sometimes you'll see a problem that doesn't contain an x, y, or z, but a hidden variable. If your answers are percents or fractional parts of some unknown quantity (total number of marbles in a jar, total miles to travel in a trip), you can still try Plugging In a number.

Read this problem:

8. In a certain high school, the number of seniors is twice the number of juniors. If 60% of the senior class and 40% of the junior class attend the last football game of the season, what percent of the combined junior and senior classes attends the game?

    (A) 60%
    (B) 53%
    (C) 50%
    (D) 47%
    (E) 40%

What number could you have that would make the math work on this problem incredibly easy? The number of students. So Plug In a number and work the problem. Suppose that the number of seniors is 200 and the number of juniors 100.

If 60% of the 200 seniors and 40% of the 100 juniors go to the game, that makes 120 seniors and 40 juniors, or 160 students. What fraction of the combined class went to the game? $\frac{160}{300}$, or 53%. So the answer is B.

Try this one:

9. Roger buys a pizza on Monday and eats $\frac{1}{5}$ that night. On Tuesday, he packs $\frac{3}{5}$ of what's left of the pizza for lunch. What fraction of the original pizza is left in his refrigerator on Tuesday?

(A) $\frac{3}{25}$

(B) $\frac{1}{5}$

(C) $\frac{8}{25}$

(D) $\frac{11}{25}$

(E) $\frac{4}{5}$

Where's the hidden variable? What is the one quantity you don't know? The number of pieces or slices in a whole pizza. So Plug In an easy number! Try 25 pieces (yes, Roger only purchases extra, extra large pizzas). How much did he eat on Monday? $\frac{1}{5}$ of 25, which works out to 5 pieces, so he must have 20 slices remaining. On Tuesday, he packs a lunch, which is $\frac{3}{5}$ of what's left, or $\frac{3}{5}$ of 20 slices, which is 12 slices. That leaves 8 slices in the fridge. Thus, the fractional part that is left in Roger's refrigerator is 8 slices out of 25 original or $\frac{8}{25}$: answer C. We picked 25 because the two fractions in the question both divide by 5, so we needed a number we could divide by 5 twice.

PLUGGING IN ON FUNCTIONS

Although function problems appear intimidating, oftentimes you can Plug In and make the problems a lot easier. Try the following problem:

18. If the $f(x) = x^2 - 2$ and $g(x) = 2x + 1$, then $f(g(x)) =$

   (A) $2x^2 - 3$
   (B) $4x^2 - 1$
   (C) $2x^2 + 2x$
   (D) $4x^2 + 2x + 1$
   (E) $4x^2 + 4x - 1$

First, Plug In an easy number for x, such as 4. Now, find the $g(4)$. Wherever there is an x, Plug In a 4.

$g(4) = 2(4) + 1 = 9$

Next, find the $f(9)$. Wherever there is an x, Plug In a 9.

$f(9) = 9^2 - 2 = 79$

Now find the answer choice that gives you 79 when you replace each x in the answer choices with the 4 you plugged in for x. The answer is E: $4(4)^2 + 4(4) - 1 = 64 + 16 - 1 = 79$. So, even though this is a number 18, it was pretty easy when you plugged in.

4. On Tuesday, Martha does $\frac{1}{2}$ of her weekly homework. On Wednesday, she does $\frac{1}{3}$ of the remaining homework. After Wednesday, what fractional part of her homework remains to be done?

(A) $\frac{1}{6}$

(B) $\frac{1}{5}$

(C) $\frac{1}{4}$

(D) $\frac{1}{3}$

(E) $\frac{1}{2}$

14. If $a = \frac{b}{c^2}$ and $c \neq \frac{1}{b^2}$, then $\frac{1}{b^2} =$

(A) ac^2

(B) a^2c^4

(C) $\frac{1}{ac^2}$

(D) $\frac{1}{a^2c^4}$

(E) $\frac{a^2}{c^4}$

17. If $p \neq 0$, then $\dfrac{\dfrac{1}{8}}{2p} =$

(A) $\dfrac{1}{4p}$

(B) $\dfrac{p}{4}$

(C) $\dfrac{4}{p}$

(D) $\dfrac{4p}{3}$

(E) $4p$

20. If $f(a, b, c) = f(c, a, b)$ for all positive numbers a, b, and c, then $f(a, b, c)$ could be which of the following functions?

(A) $a + b \neq c$

(B) $(a \times 2b \times 3c)^{(a + b + c)}$

(C) $\dfrac{ab}{c} + \dfrac{c}{ab}$

(D) $a + 2b + 3c$

(E) ab^c

Answers to Exercise 5.1

4. **D**   Plug In a number for the amount of homework Martha has. Say she has 12 pages of work to do. If she does half of this on Tuesday, she does 6 pages, and there are 6 pages left. If, on Wednesday, she does one-third of the remaining 6 pages, that means she does 2 more pages. So she has 4 pages remaining of the original 12. What fractional part is left over? $\frac{4}{12}$, or $\frac{1}{3}$.

14. **D**   Pick numbers for a, b, and c such that $a = \frac{b}{c^2}$. You can pick $4 = \frac{16}{2^2}$. Now the question becomes: what is $\frac{1}{b^2}$ or $\frac{1}{16^2}$. The answer is $\frac{1}{256}$. Plug your numbers into each answer choice. Which choice works out to be $\frac{1}{256}$? Choice D.

17. **B**   Pick a number for p. How about 2? Now the problem reads $\frac{\frac{1}{8}}{2(2)}$ and the answer is $\frac{1}{2}$. Plug your numbers into each answer choice—which one says $\frac{1}{2}$? B does.

20. **B**   This problem looks tough, but it's a snap if you Plug In. Plug In simple numbers, such as $a = 1$, $b = 1$, $c = 2$, and test to see if $f(1, 1, 2) = f(2, 1, 1)$. This is true only for B, which yields 20,736 in both cases.

PLUGGING IN THE ANSWER CHOICES

You can also Plug In when the answers to a problem are actual values, such as 2, 4, 10, or 20. Why would you want to do a lot of complicated algebra to solve a problem when the answer is right there on the page? All you have to do is figure out which choice it is.

How can you tell which is the correct answer? Try every choice until you find the one that works. Even if this means you have to try all five choices, Plugging In is still a relatively fast and reliable means of getting the right answer.

But if you use your head, you almost never have to try all five choices. When you Plug In the answer choices, begin with choice C, the middle number. If choice C works, you're done. If choice C doesn't work because it's too small, try one of the larger numbers. If choice C doesn't work because it's too big, try one of the smaller numbers. You can almost always find the answer in two or three tries.

Do the following problem:

4. If the average (arithmetic mean) of 8 and x is equal to the average of 5, 9, and x, what is the value of x ?

 (A) 1
 (B) 2
 (C) 4
 (D) 8
 (E) 10

Start with choice C and Plug In 4 for x. The problem now reads:

4. If the average (arithmetic mean) of 8 and 4 is equal to the average of 5, 9, and 4 . . .

Does this work? Is the average of 8 and 4 equal to the average of 5, 9, and 4? Yes. Therefore, C is the answer. Neat, huh?

Try one more:

10. If $(x - 2)^2 = 2x - 1$, which of the following is a possible value of x ?

(A) 1
(B) 2
(C) 3
(D) 6
(E) 7

If you try Plugging In C, 3, for x, the equation becomes $1 = 5$, which is false. So C can't be right. If you're not sure which way to go next, just pick a direction, and try the choices. It won't take very long to figure out the correct answer. If we try Plugging In B, 2, for x, the equation becomes $0 = 3$, which is false. If we try Plugging In A, 1, for x, the equation becomes $1 = 1$, which is true, so the answer is A.

Your Turn—Exercise 5.2

8. If $3^{x+2} = 243$, what is the value of x ?

(A) 1
(B) 2
(C) 3
(D) 4
(E) 5

14. If $\dfrac{24x}{4} + \dfrac{1}{x} = 5$, then $x =$

(A) $-\dfrac{1}{6}$

(B) $\dfrac{1}{6}$

(C) $\dfrac{1}{4}$

(D) $\dfrac{1}{2}$

(E) 2

Answers to Exercise 5.2

8. **C**   Begin by Plugging In the middle number, 3, for x. Is $3^5 = 243$? Yes, and the answer is C.

14. **D**   If you try Plugging In C, $\dfrac{1}{4}$, for x, the equation becomes

$\dfrac{6}{4} + 4 = 5$, which is false. If you try Plugging In D, $\dfrac{1}{2}$,

for x, the equation becomes $\dfrac{12}{4} + 2 = 5$, which is true.

Vocab Time

Turn to pages 153–154 and memorize the Hit Parade Words for Step 5.

STEP 6

WHAT ELSE DO I KNOW?: GEOMETRY

Now that you've learned the basic geometry definitions from Step 4, you're ready to tackle more complex geometry problems.

Geometry problems on the SAT are not hard because the rules of geometry are difficult; there are only a few rules, and most of them will be printed in your test booklet. (The formulas for the area of a circle, square, and triangle can be found on the first page of every Math section.) So what makes the geometry difficult on the SAT? It's that ETS doesn't simply ask you to use a formula. You almost always have to use more than one rule to solve a problem, and it's often difficult to know which rule to use first.

HINT

Whenever you see a diagram, ask yourself: What else do I know? Write everything you can think of on your booklet.

You may not see right away why it's important, but write it down anyway. Chances are good that you will be making progress toward finding the answer without even knowing it.

Here's a classic example:

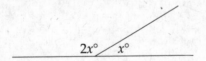

3. In the figure above, what is the value of x ?

    (A) 30
    (B) 40
    (C) 50
    (D) 60
    (E) 80

It may not be obvious to you how you should go about solving this problem. But what do you know about this diagram? You see a line, and we know that the angles on a line always add up to 180. Write that on your diagram.

Now you can see that whatever x is, the sum of angles marked $2x$ and x must equal 180. So we can write the equation $2x + x = 180$, which equals $3x = 180$, so $x = 60$. The answer is D. (You also could have plugged in the answer choices).

Try this again with the following problem:

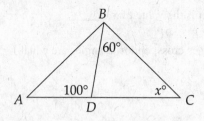

13. In triangle ABC above, $x =$

(A) 30

(B) 40

(C) 50

(D) 60

(E) 70

Notice that you don't know what angle A and angle B are. What do you know? You know that a straight line is 180 degrees, so given that angle ADB is 100 degrees, angle CDB must be 80 degrees. Knowing that angle CDB is 80, and that DBC is 60, you can figure out that angle DCB must be 40, because $80 + 60 + 40 = 180$. The answer is B, 40.

Your Turn—Exercise 6.1

(The sum of the angles that make up every line is 180 degrees.)

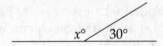

a. What is the sum of 30° and x ? _____

b. What is the value of x ? _____

(When two lines cross, opposite angles are equal.)

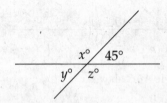

c. What is the value of x ? _____
y ? _____ z ? _____

(The sum of the angles inside every triangle is 180 degrees.)

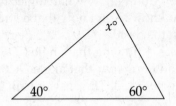

d. What is the sum of 60, 40, and x ? _____

e. What is the value of x ? _____

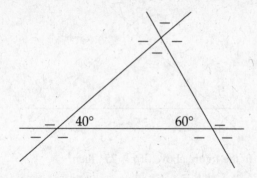

f. What are all of the angles on the above diagram?

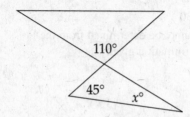

4. In the figure above, what is the value of x ?

(A) 25
(B) 30
(C) 35
(D) 40
(E) 50

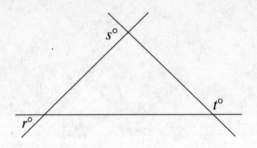

5. In the figure above, if $r = 75$, then
$r° + s° + t° = $?

(A) 25

(B) 105

(C) 255

(D) 330

(E) cannot be determined from the
information given

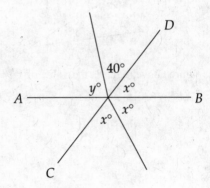

6. In the figure above, if AB and CD are
lines, what is the value of y ?

(A) 60

(B) 70

(C) 75

(D) 80

(E) 85

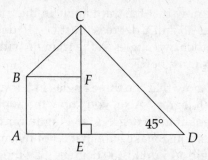

13. If the area of square $ABFE = 25$ and the area of triangle $BCF = 10$, what is the length of $\overline{ED}$?

(A) 7
(B) 8
(C) 9
(D) 10
(E) 14

Answers to Exercise 6.1

a. 180

b. 150

c. $x = 135$, $y = 45$, $z = 135$

d. 180

e. 80

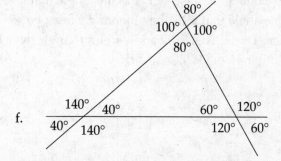

4. **A**   You know that the third angle in the triangle with angles 45 and x degrees must be 110 degrees. Because the other two angles in the triangle with x are 45 and 110, x must be 25.

5. **D**   You know that the three angles in a triangle add up to 180 degrees. Also, you know the angle opposite to r is equal to 75 degrees, so Plug In for the remaining angles—just make sure that all of the angles in the triangle add up to 180 degrees. Say the angle adjacent to s is 5 degrees and the angle adjacent to t is 100 degrees (remember, you're just making up your own numbers). That means that angle s becomes 175 degrees (with that 5-degree angle you plugged in, it forms a straight line) and angle t becomes 80 degrees. If you add up $r + s + t$, it adds up to 330 degrees, or answer D. Don't believe us? Try Plugging In some different numbers—it'll always add up to 330 degrees!

6. **D**   You know that the three angles labeled x are on a straight line, and therefore must add up to 180. Because $3x = 180$, $x = 60$. Because the angles x, 40, and y must add up to 180, and you know that $x = 60$, $60 + 40 + y = 180$, and $y = 80$.

13. **C**   If the area of the square ABFE is 25, then each of its sides must be 5. Because $\overline{BF}$ is 5, and the area of triangle BCF is 10, then side $\overline{CF}$ must be 4, making $\overline{EC}$ equal to 9. Because ECD has one angle that's 90 and one angle that's 45, the other angle must be 45 degrees. This makes ECD an isosceles triangle, which means that, if $\overline{EC}$ is 9, so is $\overline{ED}$.

Vocab Time

Turn to pages 154–155 and memorize the Hit Parade Words for Step 6.

In the next few chapters, we'll discuss some methods to help improve your score on the Critical Reading sections of the SAT. Many of these questions test your vocabulary, but even if you don't know every word, aggressive use of POE and smart guessing can help you make the most out of the vocabulary that you know.

STEP 7

SPEAK FOR YOURSELF: SENTENCE COMPLETIONS

WHAT IS A SENTENCE COMPLETION QUESTION?

Here are the instructions as you will see them on the SAT:

Each sentence below has one or two blanks, each blank indicating that something has been omitted. Beneath the sentence are five words or sets of words labeled A through E. Choose the word or set of words that, when inserted in the sentence, best fits the meaning of the sentence as a whole.

Example:

Medieval kingdoms did not become constitutional republics overnight; on the contrary, the change was _____.

(A) unpopular
(B) unexpected
(C) advantageous
(D) sufficient
(E) gradual

Most students try to solve sentence completion questions by re-reading the sentence five times, trying a different word in the blank each time, and hoping to find the one that sounds right. This is not only a waste of time (why would you want to read the sentence five times?) but it's also unhelpful. Moreover, the correct answer on a sentence completion question is not correct because of how it sounds, but because of what it means.

SPEAK FOR YOURSELF

The way to solve a sentence completion question is to try putting your own word in the blank. If you can't think of the *exact* word, think of what *kind* of word should go in the blank. Is it a positive word? A negative word? Similar to another word in the sentence? Only then should you look at the answer choices and pick the word that's closest to the word that you chose.

If you find yourself tempted to read the answer choices first, cover them up with your hand. Force yourself to figure out what the word in the blank should mean. How can you do that?

YOU'RE SMARTER THAN YOU THINK

Try this exercise: In the following sentence, what word do you think should go in the blank?

1. Susan was _____ when the formula, which had worked just yesterday, failed to produce the expected result.

What word did you put in the blank? "perplexed"? "confused"? Something of this sort has to be the word in the blank. How about this one:

2. Although she was never considered pretty as a child, Margaret grew up to be a _____ adult.

What word did you put in the blank? "beautiful"? "pretty"? "lovely"? Here you can figure out what the word in the blank has to mean, without looking at the answer choices.

Try it once more:

3. Once a cheerful person, the years of fruitless struggle against government waste made him a very_____ man.

Even if you couldn't figure out the exact word that went in the blank, you probably figured out that it had to be a word that's fairly close in meaning to "unhappy" or "bitter." That will be good enough to get the right answer, or at least to get a very good guess at the right answer.

This is why you should always approach sentence completion questions by speaking for yourself.

THE CLUE AND TRIGGER WORDS

To help you speak for yourself, learn to look for the clue and trigger words.

The Clue

How did you know what word went in the blank in the practice sentences? There is always a clue in the sentence that tells you what the word is supposed to mean.

Re-read the first example:

> **1.** Susan was _____ when the formula, which had worked just yesterday, failed to produce the expected result.

How did you know that the word had to be something like "perplexed"? Because there is a clue: "failed to produce the expected result." This tells us how Susan must feel.

Every sentence has some clue in it. Look for the clue, and it will help you determine the word that goes in the blank.

Trigger Words

Other important tools you have at your disposal are trigger words. These are words in the sentence that tell you how the word in the blank relates to the clue. For instance, look at the second sentence you tried:

> **2.** Although she was never considered pretty as a child, Margaret grew up to be a _____ adult.

How did you know that the word in the blank had to be a word like "beautiful"? Because the word "although" told you that there was a contrast in the sentence: She was never considered pretty as a child, but she *was* a pretty adult.

There are also trigger words that indicate that the word in the blank has the same meaning as the clue. For instance:

> **4.** Because Susan could not stand Jim's boorish manners, she _____ to be near him at parties.

In this case, what sort of word goes in the blank? The trigger word "because" tells you that the word in the blank will go along with the clue "could not stand Jim's boorish manners." The word in the blank must therefore be something like "hated" or "despised."

The most common **same-direction trigger words** are "and," "because," and "in fact," and the colon (:) and semi-colon (;) also act as same-direction triggers.

The most common **opposite-direction trigger words** are "but," "yet," "although," "nevertheless," "however," "once," "in spite of," and "despite." When you see these words, the word in the blank will usually mean the opposite of the clue.

When trying to find the right word for the blank, always look for the clue and trigger words. They will tell you what sort of word you need.

Here are a few sentence completion problems from which we've removed the answer choices. (You can find the complete problems with answer choices on the next page.) Read the sentence, and put your own word in the blank. Then look on the next page and see which word comes closest to the word you picked.

1. Many feature films are criticized for their _____ content, even though television news is more often the medium that depicts violent events in excessive detail.

6. In a vitriolic message to his troops, General Patton insisted that he would _____ no further insubordination, no matter how barbarous the ensuing engagements might become.

7. Chang realized that she had been _____ in her duties; had she been more vigilant, the disaster may well have been avoided.

1. Many feature films are criticized for their _____ content, even though television news is more often the medium that depicts violent events in excessive detail.

   (A) discretionary
   (B) graphic
   (C) dramatic
   (D) artistic
   (E) honest

The clue in this sentence is "even though television news is more often the medium that depicts violent events." The word in the blank should mean something like "violent." The closest word in the choices is B.

6. In a vitriolic message to his troops, General Patton insisted that he would _____ no further insubordination, no matter how barbarous the ensuing engagements might become.

   (A) impede
   (B) brief
   (C) denote
   (D) brook
   (E) expose

The clue here is "no further insubordination, no matter how." Did you pick a word like "tolerate" or "stand for" in this case? That's exactly the meaning of the word in the blank. The words in the choices are hard, but eliminate what you can and take a good guess. The answer is D.

7. Chang realized that she had been _____ in her duties; had she been more vigilant, the disaster may well have been avoided.

(A) unparalleled
(B) irreproachable
(C) derelict
(D) arbitrary
(E) punctual

The clue in this sentence is "had she been more vigilant." The word in the blank must mean the opposite of vigilant. The closest choice is C.

TWO BLANKS: TWICE AS EASY

Some of the sentence completion questions will have two blanks rather than just one. To solve these questions, do them one blank at a time. Pick one blank or the other, whichever seems easier to you, and figure out what word should go in the blank. (Often, but not always, the second blank is easier to figure out.) Then cross off all of the choices that don't work for that blank.

If more than one choice remains, pick a word for the other blank and see which of the remaining choices works best.

Read this example:

2. The scientific community was _____ when a living specimen of the coelacanth, which they feared had been _____, was discovered by deep-sea fishermen.

(A) perplexed . . common
(B) overjoyed . . dangerous
(C) unconcerned . . exterminated
(D) astounded . . extinct
(E) dismayed . . alive

The clue for the second blank is that a living specimen was found, which the scientists feared was _____. So the second blank must mean something like "destroyed." Only choices C and D are possible, so you can eliminate the others. Now look at the first blank. How did the scientists feel about the discovery? They were probably happy about it. Of C and D, which choice works with the first blank? Choice D.

SENTENCE COMPLETION SUMMARY

1. Think of your own word to fit in the blank.

2. To help you figure out the meaning of the blank, look for clues in the sentence and pay close attention to trigger words.

3. If you can't think of a precise word for the blank, at least think of what kind of word should go there. Is it a positive word? A negative word? Similar to another word in the sentence?

4. On two-blank questions, do one blank at a time.

Your Turn—Exercise 7.1

1. After the dinner, Bob sat around and _____ the new tax laws passed by Congress; he was upset and let everyone know it.

   (A) exemplified
   (B) condemned
   (C) propagated
   (D) construed
   (E) proliferated

2. Once it was revealed that Milli Vanilli had not sung the songs on their album, their _____ time in the spotlight became even more fleeting.

(A) sustained
(B) glamorous
(C) ephemeral
(D) infamous
(E) lucid

3. The employees joked that their manager was _____; even when they were deriding him in his presence, he seemed _____ and unbothered.

(A) coy . . garrulous
(B) gregarious . . reticent
(C) inept . . stoic
(D) nonplussed . . oblivious
(E) pernicious . . charmed

4. Shockingly _____ conditions exist in many of the villagers' homes, which lack electricity and indoor plumbing.

(A) wonderful
(B) primitive
(C) advanced
(D) vibrant
(E) mellifluous

5. Surprisingly, Gina was _____ to seeing the action movie, despite having professed an avid _____ for the genre.

   (A) amenable . . aversion
   (B) opposed . . antipathy
   (C) perplexed . . joy
   (D) convinced . . elation
   (E) agreeable . . pleasure

6. Madeline was always even-tempered; all of her friends were often amazed by her _____ in pressure-filled situations.

   (A) equanimity
   (B) belligerence
   (C) penitence
   (D) exquisiteness
   (E) silence

7. Blake was consistently _____ and concise, choosing to speak with fewer words than his colleagues.

   (A) verbose
   (B) obsolete
   (C) tenuous
   (D) intrepid
   (E) laconic

Answers to Exercise 7.1

1. **B** *Criticized* is a good word for the blank, because Bob was "upset about the new tax laws." "*Condemned*" is closest in meaning to *criticized*.

2. **C** According to the sentence, their career "became even more fleeting." So recycle what they've given you, and put "fleeting" in the blank. Only "ephemeral" means this.

3. **D** Do the second blank first. The boss was not bothered by his employees' derision, therefore he must've been *unbothered*. Eliminate A. Now look at the first blank; if his employees made fun of him to his face, they must joke around that he's *clueless*. Thus D is the best answer.

4. **B** Houses that lack indoor plumbing or electricity are operating in the Stone Age. Therefore, shockingly *bad* or *primitive* conditions prevail. Pick B.

5. **A** First, notice the trigger in the sentence: "despite" denotes a change of direction. Thus, the first blank is different from the second. The only answer choice that contains words that are in opposite directions is A.

6. **A** How is Madeline in high-pressure situations? Well she's always "even-tempered," so recycle this clue. The only word that means "even-tempered" is *equanimity*, or A.

7. **E** Blake is "concise" and uses very few
words. So put *not talkative* in the blank.
Which word means this? E, "laconic." If
you didn't know that, then eliminate those
words which you know do not mean
concise and take a guess. Otherwise,
study your vocabulary!

Vocab Time

Turn to pages 155–156 and memorize the Hit Parade Words for
Step 7.

LEARN THE RULES:
THE GRAMMAR SECTION

WHAT GRAMMAR RULES WILL BE TESTED?

The grammar tested on the SAT is fairly basic. You won't be expected to know a great number of obscure rules; instead, you'll be expected to know a handful of rules very well. Most of the questions on the Grammar section will test your knowledge of one or more of the following topics:

1. Verbs

   Verbs must be in agreement with their subjects, be in the proper tense, be described by adverbs, and be parallel to other verbs in the sentence.

2. Pronouns

   Pronouns must agree with the nouns they replace, be in the proper case, and unambiguously refer to only a specific noun.

3. Idioms

   Idioms are certain combinations of words and prepositions. For example, "responsible for" is an idiom. It is incorrect to say "responsible of" or "responsible to."

WHAT KINDS OF QUESTIONS ARE ON THIS TEST?

Error Identifications
Improving Sentences
Improving Paragraphs

HOW TO APPROACH ERROR IDENTIFICATIONS

Here's a sample error identification question:

Fred's <u>most</u> important chores
        A

<u>were cleaning the garage,</u> <u>to organize</u>
        B   C

his closet, and <u>washing the dishes</u>.
               D

<u>No error</u>
  E

Most students make the mistake of reading the sentence and trying to figure out what *sounds* wrong. However, this is not a very safe or efficient way of tackling these problems. Be systematic; check each underlined portion and look for major errors. Let's start by looking at one of our underlined verbs: "were." Does it agree with its subject, "chores"? Sure. Is it in the proper tense? Looks okay. Okay, so let's move on to the next verb. Is "to organize" parallel in tense with the other verbs in the series? Nope—parallel construction requires us to use the same form for all the verbs in the series. Thus, "cleaning the garage," "to organize his closet," and "washing the dishes" is incorrect. The answer is C.

Let's try another:

In the <u>class picture</u>, Tony, the <u>good-looking</u>
  A   B
track star, <u>stood</u> between you and <u>I</u>. <u>No error</u>
  C   D   E

Start with the underlined verb "stood." Is there an error in agreement, tense, or parallelism? No. Let's move on to the underlined pronoun. Check for one of the three possible pronoun errors. *I* is a subject pronoun, meaning it should be performing an action. Is *I* the subject of this sentence? No, it's actually an object of the preposition "between." We should say, "between you and me." The correct answer is D.

Your Turn—Exercise 8.1

1. <u>Although</u> the military knows how to
      A

   construct tires <u>that</u> do not need replacing,
            B

   <u>they</u> cannot sell them publicly <u>for</u> fear of
    C   D

   collapsing the tire industry. <u>No error</u>
                            E

2. The all-star team, comprised of girls from

   small, rural schools <u>scattered</u> throughout
                    A

   the state and the first such team <u>to beat</u>
                          B

   competitors from larger schools, <u>were</u> sad
                         C

   to see the tournament <u>come</u> to an end.
                     D

   <u>No error</u>
    E

3. The study revealed that in families in

   which parents were involved in <u>their</u>
                     A

   children's education, children <u>will learn</u>
                      B

   to read more easily, <u>whereas</u> when par-
                C

   ents focused on their own work, children

   tended to struggle <u>in the most</u> basic sub-
                   D

   jects. <u>No error</u>
        E

4. Sarah <u>has</u> great regard <u>to</u> Napoleon
          A   B

Bonaparte, <u>whom</u> she considers a
            C

brilliant military strategist, <u>despite</u> the
                          D

debacle at Waterloo. <u>No error</u>
                   E

5. Each of the performers <u>who</u> <u>was inducted</u>
                         A   B

into the Rock and Roll Hall of Fame

<u>has paid</u> <u>his dues</u>. <u>No error</u>
  C   D   E

6. The stage manager said that <u>even if</u> the
                            A

theatre <u>were</u> ten times bigger she still
         B

would not have enough space <u>to give</u>
                        C

each member of the cast <u>their</u> own dress-
                     D

ing room. <u>No error</u>
         E

Answers to Exercise 8.1

1. **C** The issue is pronoun agreement. The plural word "they" cannot refer to the singular word "military."

2. **C** Always check that verbs agree with their subjects. The subject of the sentence, "team," is singular, while the verb, "were," is plural.

3. **B** The sentence is in the past tense, as indicated by "revealed," and "focused." "Will learn" is in the future tense, which does not make sense in the context of the sentence.

4. **B** Idiom errors can be hard to spot. If you see an underlined preposition, there's a good chance you may have an idiom error on your hands. The correct idiom is "regard for."

5. **E** "Who" correctly refers to performers. "Each" is a singular pronoun and thus "his dues" is correct because it is also singular. The singular verb "was inducted" correctly refers to the singular subject "each," and "has paid" is the correct tense.

6. **D** Always check pronouns for agreement with the nouns they replace. The pronoun "their" (plural) refers to the noun "member" (singular).

HOW TO APPROACH IMPROVING SENTENCES

Improving sentences questions generally test the same types of rules found in the error identification questions. The only difference is that now you have to choose the answer that fixes the error. Luckily, using process of elimination is an effective tool on these kinds of questions.

Use the following guidelines when eliminating answer choices:

1. Avoid choices with the word "being" or other "-ing" verbs.

2. Avoid choices that contain ambiguous pronouns.

3. Avoid choices that change the meaning of the sentence.

4. Avoid choices that are excessively wordy.

HINT

Answer choice (A) is no error.

Your Turn—Exercise 8.2

On the following sentences try to eliminate as many answers as possible using the rules above.

1. In order to look sideways, owls must turn their entire heads: their eyes are directed forward and are encased in a capsule of <u>bone where little eye movement is allowed</u>.

   (A) bone where little eye movement is allowed

   (B) bone, which is allowing little eye movement

   (C) bone, when allowing little eye movement

   (D) bone that allows little eye movement

   (E) bone with eye movement not allowed

2. At the recent opening of the college's production of *Hedda Gabler*, the audience watched the play enraptured <u>and, when the curtains came down, they applauded for at least ten minutes</u>.

   (A) and, when the curtains came down, they applauded for at least ten minutes

   (B) and it applauded for at least ten minutes, the curtains having come down

   (C) and, when the curtains came down, they were applauding for at least ten minutes

   (D) and, when the curtains came down, applauded for at least ten minutes

   (E) and for at least ten minutes they applauded when the curtains came down

Answers to Exercise 8.2

1. **D** Eliminate choices B and C because they contain "-ing" verbs. E changes the meaning of the sentence so you can eliminate it as well. If you're down to two choices, pick the shorter (or less wordy) one.

2. **D** B and C should be eliminated because they both contain "ing" words. Eliminate A and E because they both use the ambiguous pronoun "they."

MODIFIER AND COMPARISON ERRORS

In addition to errors involving verbs, pronouns, and idioms, improving sentences questions also feature errors involving modifiers and comparisons.

In the following sentence, the phrase in italics is the modifier:

Never seen alive in its native habitat, scientists are desperately seeking information on the reclusive giant squid.

This sentence is incorrect as written because the modifier should refer to the giant squid but the noun following the modifier is "scientists." Make sure the modified noun follows directly after the modifying phrase.

Try the following problem:

6. Signed in Mexico City on February 2, 1848, the boundaries of the United States were extended by The Treaty of Guadalupe Hidalgo.

    (A) the boundaries of the United States were extended by The Treaty of Guadalupe Hidalgo

    (B) the United States' boundaries were extended by the Treaty of Guadalupe Hidalgo

    (C) the United States extended its boundaries by the Treaty of Guadalupe Hidalgo

    (D) the Treaty of Guadalupe Hidalgo extended the boundaries of the United States

    (E) the Treaty of Guadalupe Hidalgo was extended by the boundaries of the United States

In this sentence, the modifying phrase is "Signed in Mexico City on February 2, 1848." However, the noun directly following it is "the boundaries of the United States." Clearly, the boundaries weren't signed in 1848. Eliminate A, B, and C. Eliminate E based on common sense: A treaty cannot be extended by a boundary. The correct answer is D.

When a sentence makes a comparison, check that the two things being compared are parallel, or in other words, that the sentence repeats similar grammatical structure. For example, this sentence contains a faulty comparison:

> The texture and gloss of an oil painting is far different from acrylic.

This sentence is purporting to compare an oil *painting* to an acrylic *painting*. Unfortunately, as written, the sentence compares an oil *painting* to *acrylic*.

Try this one:

4. The sound system in Doug's car is both <u>more expensive and more powerful than Jamie's car</u>.

   (A) more expensive and more powerful than Jamie's car

   (B) more expensive and more powerful than the one found in Jamie's car

   (C) more expensive and more powerful than Jamie

   (D) more expensive and more powerful than Jamie's

   (E) more expensive and more powerful than the sound system in Jamie's car

Did you spot the faulty comparison? We need to compare Doug's sound system to Jamie's sound system, not to her car. E makes this comparison in the clearest and most concise way.

Your Turn—Exercise 8.3

1. <u>Documented in a special collection at the Library of Congress Music Division, Leonard Bernstein, composer, conductor, writer, and teacher, led an extraordinary life.</u>

    (A) Documented in a special collection at the Library of Congress Music Division, Leonard Bernstein, composer, conductor, writer, and teacher, led an extraordinary life.

    (B) Documented in a special collection at the Library of Congress Music Division, Leonard Bernstein led an extraordinary life as a composer, conductor, writer, and teacher.

    (C) Leonard Bernstein's extraordinary life as a composer, conductor, writer, and teacher is documented in a special collection at the Library of Congress Music Division.

    (D) Documented in a special collection at the Library of Congress Music Division, Leonard Bernstein, composer, conductor, writer, and teacher, is the subject of the collection.

    (E) Documented in a special collection at the Library of Congress Music Division, Leonard Bernstein is portrayed as having an extraordinary life as a composer, conductor, writer, and teacher.

2. The art of Pablo Picasso, whose paintings are considered by many to be modern masterpieces, <u>is admired not only for its innovative content but also for its</u> mastery of form.

(A) is admired not only for its innovative content but also for its

(B) is admired not only for its innovative content and also for its

(C) are admired not only for their innovative content but also for their

(D) are admired not for their innovative content only; also for their

(E) is admired not only for its innovative content than for its

3. The featured selection in this month's catalogue <u>was advertised for its high quality, low cost, and how easy it is to use and store</u>.

(A) was advertised for its high quality, low cost, and how easy it is to use and store

(B) was advertised for its high quality, low cost, and its ease of use and storage

(C) has been advertised for its high quality, low cost, and how easy it is to use and store

(D) has been advertised for its high quality, low cost, and ease of both use and storage

(E) was advertised for its high quality, low cost, and ease of use and storage

4. <u>Vibrissae, the scientific term for the whiskers of a cat, is sensitive so that</u> they can detect the slightest change in air currents.

(A) Vibrissae, the scientific term for the whiskers of a cat, is sensitive so that

(B) So sensitive are the scientific term for a cat's whiskers, vibrissae, that

(C) The scientific term for a cat's whiskers, vibrissae, is so sensitive

(D) Vibrissae, the scientific term for a cat's whiskers, are so sensitive that

(E) A cat's whiskers, the scientific term for them being vibrissae, are so sensitive

5. <u>Although set in different locales, the operettas of Gilbert and Sullivan, like the novels of Jane Austen, have similar plots and often recycle stock characters.</u>

(A) Although set in different locales, the operettas of Gilbert and Sullivan, like the novels of Jane Austen, have similar plots and often recycle stock characters.

(B) Although they are set in different locales, Gilbert and Sullivan, like Jane Austen, have similar plots and often recycle stock characters.

(C) Although set in different locales, Gilbert and Sullivan, as well as Jane Austen, have similar plots, often recycling stock characters.

(D) Although being set in different locales, the operettas of Gilbert and Sullivan, like the novels of Jane Austen, have similar plots and having recycled stock characters.

(E) Although they take place in different settings, the operettas of Gilbert and Sullivan, like the novels of Jane Austen, have similar plots because they often recycle stock characters.

6. Although the meals at Eli's Saucy Seafood were tasty, <u>Ron's Bulkhead was an outstanding restaurant</u>.

(A) Ron's Bulkhead was an outstanding restaurant

(B) Ron's Bulkhead had a better atmosphere

(C) the entrees at Ron's Bulkhead were infinitely better

(D) Ron's Bulkhead is an outstanding restaurant

(E) the entrees that are infinitely better are the ones at Ron's Bulkhead

Answers to Exercise 8.3

1. **C** Only choice C corrects the misplaced modifier created in the original sentence. The long descriptive phrase at the beginning of the sentence *Documented in a special collection at the Library of Congress Music Division* is not describing Leonard Bernstein.

2. **A** The sentence is correct as written. The singular subject "art" matches the singular verb "is", and "not only" is correctly paired with "but also." Answer choices B and E improperly match "not only" with "and" and "than" respectively. Choices C and D incorrectly use plural verbs.

3. **E** Choice E correctly maintains parallel structure. Choices A and B lack parallelism and therefore are eliminated. Choices C and D are incorrect because they use the wrong verb tense.

4. **D** Choices A and B contain a subject-verb error. Choice B further incorrectly implies that the scientific term for a cat's whiskers, rather than the whiskers themselves, can detect changes in air currents, as does choice C. Choice E contains the awkward and unnecessary "ing" word "being."

5. **A** The sentence is correct as written. "Although set in different locales" modifies the operettas, not Gilbert and Sullivan themselves, making choices B and C incorrect. Choice D incorrectly uses "ing" words "being set" and "having recycled." Choice E improperly makes a causal connection.

6. **C** Choice C correctly compares the meals at Eli's with the meals at Ron's. Choices A, B, and D incorrectly compare the meals at Eli's with various characteristics of Ron's Bulkhead, not the meals themselves and therefore are eliminated. You are left with C and E. Pick the shorter one.

HOW TO APPROACH IMPROVING PARAGRAPHS

In the improving paragraphs portion of the Writing section, you will be tested on your use of standard written English. These questions are designed to measure your ability to recognize errors and improve sentences and paragraphs in context. Here's a sample:

> (1) *Internet cookies are a controversial topic in the computer world.* (2) *When you visit a website such as a travel website it might put a cookie on your computer to mark that website.* (3) *That mark tells the Internet that you are interested in travel.* (4) *The Internet tailors its advertising on websites you visit based on your interests so you would see a lot more ads for travel sites and discount flights.* (5) *But is this good or bad?*

> (6) *Some people don't mind having cookies on their computer.* (7) *They think that if they have to see advertising that it might as well be relevant.* (8) *And sometimes a person interested in travel will click on that ad to learn more about the service offered and after all advertising is a big business and it works because people respond to it.*

> (9) *Other people expunge cookies immediately.* (10) *They do not want the Internet marking their computers with their preferences.* (11) *Some may fear that their government or school is policing their right to access information.* (12) *These people prefer their privacy to learning about websites and expunge cookies immediately.*

> (13) *Depending on your personality, you might enjoy cookies or not.* (14) *Whichever your preference, you should be aware that they exist and that they have an impact on your computer when you access the Internet.*

Hopefully you didn't spend a lot of time reading this essay and trying to comprehend the information in it. That's not the goal of these questions. Instead of reading thoroughly, quickly skim the essay. We want to spend our time on the questions, not on the passage.

QUESTION TYPES

Improving paragraph questions generally come in three varieties:

1. Revision questions

    These questions ask about a sentence that contains some sort of grammatical error, similar to those found in error identifications and improving sentences. You will be asked to fix the sentence or to make the sentence clearer.

2. Combination questions

    These questions require you to join two sentences together.

3. Content questions

    Some questions may ask you to add a sentence, remove a sentence, or find the main idea of the passage.

Let's try a few.

1. In context, which of the following is the best revision of sentence 5 (reproduced below)?

    But is this good or bad?

    (A) But is the use of cookies beneficial or not?
    (B) But are these websites helpful or harmful?
    (C) But is the Internet a positive or a negative force?
    (D) But is an interest in travel healthy or unhealthy?
    (E) But are computers good or evil?

This sentence appears a bit vague. Let's go back to the passage and read a few sentences before sentence 5 to get a sense of the topic. The passage is discussing cookies, so the best answer should make this clear. The only choice that does so is A.

2. In context, which word should be placed at the beginning of sentence 4 (reproduced below)?

The Internet tailors its advertising on websites you visit based on your interests so you would see a lot more ads for travel sites and discount flights.

(A) Nevertheless

(B) Although

(C) Subsequently

(D) Because

(E) However

Again, go back to the passage and see how sentence 4 relates to the sentences around it. Sentence 3 introduces an idea and sentence 4 develops it. Which word best indicates a continuation of the idea? It looks like choice C is best.

3. The writer's main rhetorical purpose of the essay is to

(A) analyze how cookies interact with travel websites

(B) prove that cookies individualize one's Internet experience in a positive way

(C) show how cookies compromise our constitutional freedoms

(D) theorize on how personalities affect computer usage

(E) describe cookies and the controversy surrounding them

Save questions about the content of the passage as a whole for last. Usually you will have a good sense of the main idea after answering the other more specific questions. If not, read the topic sentences of each paragraph and the final line of the entire passage to gain a sense of the main idea. Based on the questions we've answered so far, can you eliminate any answer choices? Right off the bat, eliminate D because that choice doesn't even mention cookies. From question 1, we know that the author isn't sure if cookies are good or bad, so let's eliminate B and C. Is the entire passage about travel websites? A quick skim shows that travel websites are mentioned only briefly. Thus, E is the best answer.

Your Turn—Exercise 8.4

(1) *Costa Rica became independent in 1821, with democratic elections later that century, actually establishing its constitution in 1949.* (2) *It has become one of the most inviting Central American countries for United States tourists as well as Europe.*

(3) *Visitors enjoy the culture and the economy that has become strong partly in regards to tourism.* (4) *Travelers prefer to visit countries that are politically stable, which is, unlike some Central and South American countries, generally true here.* (5) *Yet surrounded by the Caribbean Sea and the Pacific Ocean boasts more than 750 miles of coastline with great beaches.*

(6) *The "dry season" is December through April.* (7) *It is the dry season, there is almost no rain.* (8) *Excepting, on the Caribbean coast.* (9) *The rest of the year, the "rainy season" which locals call the "green season," is great for travel too.* (10) *The rain is not necessarily constant.* (11) *On the northwest coast it rains only for part of not every day.* (12) *Temperatures remain basically steady all year.* (13) *In the mountains that run through the middle of Costa Rica, the lows average around 60 degrees Fahrenheit with highs around 80; on the coasts the temperature ranges from about 70 to around 90.*

(14) *Costa Rica's specialty is "ecotourism," or tourism for viewing forests, wildlife, rivers, etc.* (15) *Costa Rica's mountains include active volcanoes and volcanic craters.* (16) *Between there and the ocean are rain forests and cloud forests, high-altitude rain forests with clouds throughout, all with amazing animals, plants, and insects.* (17) *And even the coastline, known for beaches, have waterfalls, rare birds, and turtles.*

1. In context, which of the following is the best way to revise sentence 1?

    (A) (as it is now)

    (B) Costa Rica became independent in 1821, with democratic elections later, actually establishing its constitution in 1949.

    (C) With Costa Rica becoming independent in 1821, holding democratic elections later that century, and actually establishing its constitution in 1949.

    (D) With Costa Rica becoming independent in 1821, democratic elections later that century, and actually establishing its constitution in 1949.

    (E) Costa Rica became independent in 1821, held democratic elections later that century, and actually established its constitution in 1949.

2. In the context of the passage as a whole, which of the following is the best way to phrase the underlined portion of sentence 5 (reproduced below)?

Yet surrounded by the Caribbean Sea and the Pacific Ocean boasts more than 750 miles of coastline with great beaches.

(A) Furthermore, being surrounded by the Caribbean Sea as well as the Pacific Ocean on the other side, boasts

(B) Yet surrounded by the Caribbean and Pacific Oceans, Costa Rica boasts

(C) For example, it is surrounded by the Caribbean Sea and the Pacific Ocean, which boast

(D) In addition, Costa Rica, surrounded by the Caribbean Sea and Pacific Ocean, boasts

(E) Yet, surrounded by the Caribbean Sea and Pacific Ocean, Costa Rica is boasting

3. In context, which of the following represents the best way to revise and combine sentences 7 and 8 (reproduced below)?

It is the dry season, there is almost no rain. Excepting, on the Caribbean coast.

(A) During this season, almost no rain falls, even on the Caribbean coast.

(B) During this season, almost no rain falls, except on the Caribbean coast.

(C) During the dry season, there is almost no rain on the Caribbean coast.

(D) During the dry season, there is almost no rain, with the exception being the coast of the Caribbean.

(E) During the dry season, almost no rain is going to fall anywhere, excepting on the Caribbean coast.

4. The logical flow of the passage as a whole would be most improved by making which of the following changes to the third paragraph?

(A) After sentence 13, insert a sentence providing examples of low and high temperatures in specific cities.

(B) After sentence 13, insert a sentence citing instances when violent and dangerous storms have struck Costa Rica during the rainy season.

(C) After sentence 12, insert a sentence stating the name and highest elevation of the mountain range in central Costa Rica.

(D) Before sentence 11, insert a sentence noting that during the rainy season, roads may be washed out.

(E) Before sentence 6, insert a sentence explaining that the weather in Costa Rica is one of its primary appeals for tourists.

5. Which of the following represents the best revision, in context, of the underlined part of sentence 17 (reproduced below)?

And even the coastline, known for beaches, have waterfalls, rare birds, and turtles.

(A) Even the coastline, known for its beaches, has

(B) And so the coastline, known for its beaches, even has

(C) Even the coastline, which is known for its beaches, having

(D) And even the coastline, typically known for its beaches, having

(E) And, the coastline itself, which is known for its beaches, even have

ANSWERS TO EXERCISE 8.4

1. **E** The verbs "became" and "establishing" are not parallel, so the sentence is flawed as written and choice A is incorrect. Choice B is incorrect for the same reason and because removing "that century" makes the sentence less clear. Choices C and D feature parallel verbs but neither one expresses a complete thought and both use "ing" verbs, so both are incorrect. Choice E is a complete sentence with parallel verbs "became," "held," and "established"; thus it is the credited answer.

2. **D** Sentence 5 is a fragment as written. Choice A does not correct this problem because it does not include a clear subject. Also, sentence 5 is an extension of the list of reasons why tourists find Costa Rica appealing, so it needs to begin with a word that shows this relationship. Hence, choices B and E, which begin with "Yet," are incorrect. Choice C replaces the verb "boasts" with the phrase "which boast" and thus changes the meaning of the sentence by suggesting that these waters, rather than Costa Rica, boast more than 750 miles of coastline. Choice D makes the sentence complete without changing its meaning, and it also refers to the waters concisely as "the Caribbean Sea and Pacific Ocean."

3. **B** In context, the phrase "the dry season" is unnecessarily wordy; "this season" is sufficiently clear. The phrases "there is almost no rain" and "almost no rain falls" bear the same meaning, so again the more concise phrasing is better. For these reasons, eliminate choices C and D. Choice E is even wordier, so it can be eliminated as well. Although choice A is more efficient, the word "even," which appears in place of "excepting," changes the meaning of the sentence, so choice A is incorrect.

4. **E** The general theme of this passage as a whole is to explain Costa Rica's tourist appeal, and this paragraph largely focuses on the country's inviting weather. Choices B and D undermine this message by providing specific negative information, so both are incorrect. Choices A and C suggest

adding details that would not specifically contribute to the implied focus of the second paragraph. Choice E suggests adding a topic sentence that would not only be consistent with the general purpose of this paragraph but would clarify that purpose in a valuable way.

5. **A** The subject of this sentence is "coastline" (singular), so the verb "have" (plural) is incorrect. Thus, choice E is wrong. Replacing "have" with "having" does not improve the sentence because doing so creates a sentence fragment; hence, choices C and D are incorrect. Nothing in the context suggests a cause and effect relationship here, so choice B, which includes "so," is incorrect as well. Furthermore, "And" is grammatically incorrect as used in choices B and D and unnecessary in choice E. In choice A, "And" has been eliminated, and the sentence features the correct verb form, "has."

GRAMMAR SUMMARY

1. Keep your eyes open for the most common types of errors. Make sure you know what types of errors can occur with verbs, pronouns, and idioms.

2. Make aggressive use of process of elimination. Even if you are not sure what the right answer is, eliminate any choices that you know to be wrong and take a guess.

3. Use the rules you've learned for error identifications and improving sentences to help you on the improving paragraph questions.

Vocab Time

Turn to pages 156–157 and memorize the Hit Parade Words for Step 8.

TREASURE HUNT:
CRITICAL READING

CRITICAL READING—SHORT AND LONG PASSAGES

You will encounter two types of critical reading passages on the test— short reading passages that average 10–15 lines of text and long reading passages that average about 70–80 lines of text.

In either case, the directions are the same:

> The passage below is followed by questions based on its content. Answer the questions on the basis of what is <u>stated</u> or <u>implied</u> in the passage and in any introductory material that may be provided.

You might think that this means that you need to read the passage carefully, understand it thoroughly, or make complex inferences from the information contained in the passage. You don't.

Think of critical reading as a treasure hunt: All the answers to the questions are buried somewhere in the passage. All you've got to do is find them.

APPROACHING CRITICAL READING

The problem with critical reading questions is, of course, that these passages are boring, dense, brutish, and long. How can you get the most points in the least amount of time, and in the most reliable way? Well, not by reading the whole passage carefully. You can do it by knowing where to find the answer quickly within the passage, and then finding the choice that restates what is said in the passage.

An Encyclopedia

If someone were to give you a ten-volume encyclopedia and ask you the year of Pasteur's death, would you begin reading at the A's and work all the way through to the P's until you found Pasteur? Of course not. You'd go right to the entry on Pasteur and read only the five or six lines that you need. That's how you should approach critical reading questions.

Your Treasure Hunt

So here are the steps to finding your answers in the most efficient way:

1. Go to the questions. Do the line-specific questions first and the general questions later.

2. Put the question in your own words.

3. Find the answer to the question in the passage.

4. Pick the answer choice that comes closest to what you found in the passage.

SPECIFIC QUESTIONS

Many critical reading questions will be line-specific questions. That is, they will ask you for facts from particular parts of the passage. Some of those ask you for the definition of words.

To answer any line-specific question, the method is the same. Hunt for the answer in the passage using the clues in the question, read that area of the passage to find the answer to the question, and then pick the answer choice that is the best paraphrase of what the passage says.

The most common kinds of line-specific questions are line number and vocabulary in context questions:

- **Line number questions:** If the question gives you a line reference, go back to the passage and read that line in context (from about three to five lines before the line reference, to three to five lines following the line reference). Then, find the choice that restates what is said in these lines.

- **Vocabulary in context questions:** If the question asks you to define a word, treat the question like a sentence completion. Go back to the sentence in which the word occurs and cross it out. Then, read the sentence and pick your own word to put in its place. This will give you an idea of what the word should mean. (Be careful, because the word in question may not have the meaning that's most familiar to you!)

Then, look for the choice that best states what you think the word means in context.

POE on Specific Questions

There are two important rules of thumb on specific questions:

- Avoid extremes
- Avoid offense

ETS does not pick extreme or offensive passages for its tests. If you see a choice that's very extreme (extreme choices sometimes use words such as *must, always, only, every*) or potentially very offensive to a certain class of people, eliminate it.

Here are some examples of choices that you can eliminate:

- judges deliberately undermine the constitution
- doctors are the only people who can cure malaria
- it was entirely misleading
- disparage the narrow-mindedness of modern research
- all his beliefs about his parents were wrong

Likewise, for questions that ask you about the author's attitude or tone, eliminate extremes, such as:

- sarcasm
- ridicule
- repugnance
- condemnation

Your Turn—Exercise 9.1

Try answering the questions following the short reading passage below.

Sleep deprivation experts have suggested a link
between the amount of sleep a person gets and the
likelihood of being overweight. A study conducted in
Line Japan compared seven- and eight-year-olds who slept
5   nine or more hours per night to those who slept fewer
hours than that. Those who slept eight hours were
twice as likely to have weight problems than those who
slept nine or more hours per night. The children who
slept less than eight hours were four times as likely to
10 be obese than those who slept nine or more hours per
night. One theory suggested by dieticians to explain
this data is that sleep deprivation affects hormone levels. Another theory is that people who lack sleep eat
high-sugar foods during the day for energy, and may
15 generally be lethargic due to a lack of energy.

1. The study cited in lines 3–6 ("A study...
    that.") serves primarily to
    (A) explain how hormone levels affect
        weight gain
    (B) indicate why some children lack
        energy
    (C) support the proposal in the first sen-
        tence
    (D) establish evidence to prove the theory
        in the last sentence
    (E) warn Americans not to oversleep

2. It can be most strongly inferred from the passage that

(A) increased sleep induces weight loss

(B) people should sleep ten hours per night

(C) dieticians have determined the causes of obesity

(D) some Japanese children are overweight

(E) many Japanese children do not get enough sleep

Answers to Exercise 9.1

1. **C**   The study provides evidence that there might be a link, as stated in the first sentence. Because the passage does not explain the relationship between hormone levels and weight gain, answer choice A can be eliminated. Eliminate choice B because the study never addressed why some children lacked energy. While choice D is tempting, the theory is presented in the passage as a way to explain the study, not the other way around. Eliminate choice E because, based on the study, sleeping longer appears to be beneficial, not something to be warned against.

2. **D** Because the study was conducted in Japan, and some of those children were used to demonstrate the link between obesity and sleep, it can be inferred that some Japanese children are overweight. Eliminate choice A because while decreased sleep might be linked to weight gain, it doesn't follow that increased sleep induces weight loss. While choice B is tempting, eliminate it because there is no evidence that all people should sleep ten hours per night, only that those who slept more than nine hours were less likely to become obese. Choice C is incorrect because the dieticians present at least two theories to explain obesity, but have not determined the causes. Choice E is incorrect because "enough sleep" is not defined in the passage.

GENERAL QUESTIONS

You may see one or two general questions that ask you for the main point or primary purpose of the passage. Save these for last; after answering the line-specific questions, you'll almost always have a good sense of the main idea. If you're stuck, try rereading the first and last lines of every paragraph, and any line that contains a trigger word (*but, yet, although, nevertheless, however*). These are the most important lines in the passage, and you will most likely find the main idea in these lines.

POE on General Questions

The two biggest pitfalls to avoid on general questions are:

- too specific
- impossible to accomplish

Choices that are discussed only in one part of the passage are too specific to be the main point. The main point of a passage is something that relates to the passage as a whole. Also, use common sense: Any choice that is impossible to accomplish in a couple of paragraphs (such as "prove that comets killed the dinosaurs") can't be the answer to a general question.

DUAL PASSAGE

One section of the SAT will probably contain a dual passage, that is, two passages that have differing viewpoints on a common theme. Following the passages will be some questions that are relevant to only one passage or the other, and some questions that ask you to compare the two passages. These comparison questions are usually harder, so the best strategy is:

1. Read the blurb for Passage 1.

2. Answer the questions on Passage 1.

3. Read the blurb for Passage 2.

4. Answer the questions on Passage 2.

5. Answer any questions that ask you to compare the two passages.

This way, you'll save the hardest problems for last—and if you run out of time, you can skip them entirely.

Try these techniques on the following passage:

John Dewey was an American educator and thinker. In the following excerpt from Democracy and Education, *he explains why education is necessary for human beings.*

The most notable distinction between living and inanimate things is that the former maintain themselves by renewal. A stone when struck resists. If its

Line resistance is greater than the force of the blow struck,
5 it remains outwardly unchanged. Otherwise, it is shattered into smaller bits. Never does the stone attempt to react in such a way that it may maintain itself against the blow, much less so as to render the blow a contributing factor to its own continued action. While
10 the living thing may easily be crushed by superior force, it nonetheless tries to turn the energies that act upon it into means of its own further existence. If it cannot do so, it does not just split into smaller pieces (at least in the higher forms of life), but loses its iden-
15 tity as a living thing. As long as it endures, the living thing struggles to use surrounding energies in its own behalf. It uses light, air, moisture, and the material of soil. Life is a self-renewing process through action upon the environment.

20 With the renewal of physical existence goes, in the case of human beings, the recreation of beliefs, ideals, hopes, happiness, misery, and practices. The continuity of any experience, through renewing of the social group, is a literal fact. Education, in its broadest
25 sense, is the means of this social continuity of life. Every one of the constituent elements of a social group, in a modern city as in a savage tribe, is born immature, helpless, without language, beliefs, ideas, or social standards. Each individual, each unit who is
30 the carrier of the life-experience of his group, in time passes away. Yet the life of the group goes on.

The primary ineluctable facts of the birth and death of each one of the constituent members in a social group determine the necessity of education. Even in a
35 savage tribe, the achievements of adults are far beyond what the immature members would be capable of if

left to themselves. With the growth of civilization, the gap between the original capacities of the immature and the standards and customs of the elders increases.
40 Mere physical growing up, mere mastery of the bare necessities of subsistence will not suffice to reproduce the life of the group. Deliberate effort and the taking of thoughtful pains are required. Beings who are born not only unaware of, but quite indifferent to, the aims
45 and habits of the social group have to be rendered cognizant of them and actively interested. Education, and education alone, spans the gap.

Society exists through a process of transmission quite similar to biological life. Without this communication
50 of ideals, hopes, expectations, standards, opinions, from those members of society who are passing out of the group life to those who are coming into it, social life could not survive. If the members who compose a society lived on continuously, they might educate the new-born
55 members, but it would be a task directed by personal interest rather than social need. Now it is a work of necessity. If a plague carried off the members of a society all at once, it is obvious that the group would be permanently done for. Yet the death of each of its constituent
60 members is as certain as if an epidemic took them all at once. But the graded difference in age, the fact that some are born as some die, makes possible through transmission of ideas and practices the constant reweaving of the social fabric. Yet this renewal is not automatic. Unless
65 pains are taken to see that genuine and thorough transmission takes place, the most civilized group will relapse into barbarism and then into savagery.

1. The author discusses a stone (lines 3–9)
in order to explain

(A) the forces necessary to destroy rock

(B) the difference between living and
non-living beings

(C) why living things cannot be split into
pieces

(D) why living things are easier to crush
than stones

(E) the nutritional requirements for life

The stone is an example that illustrates something. What
does it illustrate? Read three to five lines above (in this case,
from the beginning of the passage) to three to five lines below
the example, and look for the idea supported by the case
of the stone. The answer is in the first line: the "distinction
between living and inanimate things is that the former maintain themselves by renewal." Which choice paraphrases this
line? B does.

2. The primary purpose of the passage is to

(A) argue that we should spend more
money on public schools

(B) explain why the author wants to be a
teacher

(C) prove that humans would die without education

(D) recount the author's own experience
as a student

(E) support the claim that good education is essential for human beings

Because this is a general question, save it for last. Not only is the blurb a good clue to the main point, but notice that many of the questions revolve around the question of education. Choice A might be something that the author believes, but public schools are never mentioned in the passage. Choice C is simply too big a task to be accomplished in a short passage. Choices B and D are too personal; the author never discusses his own memories or wishes. The best choice is E.

3. The word "ineluctable" as used in line 32 most nearly means

 (A) unhappy
 (B) absurd
 (C) unchangeable
 (D) indifferent
 (E) proven

Cross off the word "ineluctable" on line 32, reread the line, and pick your own word to go in the blank. The word that fills the blank must be something like "unavoidable" or "certain." Which choice comes closest in meaning? Choice C does.

4. According to the passage, the "necessity of education" (line 34) is based in the fact that humans

 (A) have mothers and fathers
 (B) have larger brains than any other animal
 (C) are more advanced than other animals
 (D) are mortal
 (E) are born unable to feed themselves

Reread line 34 in context to see what the passage says. It states that "the primary ineluctable facts of the birth and death of each one of the constituent members in a social group determine the necessity of education." Which choice is the best paraphrase of this line? Because humans are born and die—that is, because they are mortal—explains the necessity of education. So the answer is D.

5. The author implies, in the last paragraph, that without a concerted effort to educate the young, humans

   (A) will become extinct
   (B) may return to a more savage lifestyle
   (C) would not be as happy as those with education
   (D) will become more like stones
   (E) may have poorly behaved children

In the very last sentence of the passage, the author claims that "unless pains are taken to see that genuine and thorough transmission takes place, the most civilized group will relapse into barbarism and then into savagery." What choice paraphrases this line? B does.

Vocab Time
Turn to pages 158–159 and memorize the Hit Parade Words for Step 9.

STEP 10

WRITING 101:
THE ESSAY

WHAT MAKES A GOOD ESSAY?

Your English teacher might have a very different answer to this question, but for the purposes of the SAT, a good essay is one that makes the job of the essay graders an easy one. Put yourself in the place of the poor SAT essay graders. They have to spend all day cooped up in a stuffy room with hundreds of other graders, reading through thousands of student essays, all on the same topic. It's not the best way to spend a weekend.

So let's make sure that when the essay graders read your essay, it's easy for them to give you a top score. The first and most important thing to realize is that your essay is graded holistically—meaning that the readers assign a grade based on the overall impression of the essay. In fact, the graders on average will spend only about two minutes reading your essay and will only read your essay once. So there's no time to examine every little aspect of your writing. In that short amount of time, the reader can only look for a couple of major characteristics.

WHAT ARE THE GRADERS LOOKING FOR?

When your graders read your essay, they are looking for the following:

1. Did you address the prompt?

    The prompts are designed to give you some degree of flexibility in how you respond to them. However, your essay still has to address the prompt, even if only tangentially.

2. Did you organize your thoughts?

    In 25 minutes, you don't have a lot of time to plan your essay. And there is no time to rewrite your essay if need be. But, you should still be able to write an organized essay with an introduction, body paragraphs, and a conclusion.

3. Did you use examples to support your thesis?

   This is an absolute must. You have to use examples in your essay.

4. Did you avoid grammatical mistakes and other stylistic errors?

   It's okay to have a couple of grammar mistakes or misspellings. You can still get a top score. But if you have a lot of these errors, they will lessen the overall impression of your essay and thus hurt your score.

Let's address each of these topics in-depth.

THE PROMPT

The prompt is designed to elicit a variety of responses. There is no "right" or "wrong" response, so don't worry about the nature of your take on the prompt. The prompt itself will likely be an excerpt from a literary work. Here's an example:

> Upon considering all the evidence—the effect of parents and siblings, the influence of society, the weight of religion, the impact of school and trade—it is clear that we humans are indeed created as blank slates. Born innocent and free from any predetermined personality characteristics, we develop and nurture our personalities through our interactions with the world around us. Were we to grow up in an environment devoid of institutions, our character would be likewise empty.
>
> Are we essentially a blank slate? Plan and write an essay in which you develop your point of view on this issue. Support your position with reasoning and examples taken from your reading, studies, experience, or observations.

After reading the prompt, first decide what your response will be. In general, you will most likely:

1. Agree with the prompt.

2. Agree with the prompt, but with certain reservations.

3. Disagree with the prompt.

4. Disagree with the prompt, but with certain reservations.

Of course, if you have a different response, that's fine as well. The main point is to come up with a definitive thesis. Having a clear focus for your essay will make it easier to write and organize. Once you've decided what your thesis will be, you're ready to write your introductory paragraph.

NOW INTRODUCING...

Now that you know your thesis and your examples, it's time to start writing. The general structure for the essay should be: introduction, two examples, and conclusion. If you have two really solid, detailed, relevant examples, stick to those. Don't throw in a third because you think you have to.

With your introduction, you want to state your point of view clearly. Your entire essay has to connect back to your thesis, so make sure that your thesis is stated directly. Your goal is to state that you agree or disagree with the assignment.

Don't just state that you agree or disagree, of course. Restate "I agree" or "I disagree" as a full sentence, such as "You should focus on your own good, which can help others," or "It is better to focus on the good of others rather than on yourself."

Once you've stated your thesis, you can elaborate a little bit. You'll use specific examples later on, so for now just explain why you believe what you do. Something such as "People know what is best for themselves better than they know what is better for others," or "Civilization is built on the fact that people help others over themselves." Emphasize the point you've made with your thesis; don't confuse it.

You want to finish your introduction by previewing the examples you're going to talk about. This shows your reader that you've organized your thoughts. Otherwise it looks as though you're just rambling on without evidence, and maybe without a point!

Here is a sample introductory paragraph:

Human beings are not blank slates, waiting to be filled with information. There are many instances in which a person develops a personality or characteristics completely at odds with the environment or social structure in which he or she grew up. Nelson Mandela's quest for equality and Gandhi's mission of peace both show how individuals can have radically different views and methods from the society that rears them.

Your Turn—Exercise 10.1

Now you try it. Using the prompt below, write an introductory paragraph.

> What is justice? How would one define justice, or even know it? Classical wisdom presents many examples of justice, but few definitions. The problem with defining justice seems to lie in the subjectivity of the participants. Does the criminal sentenced to a lengthy term feel that the sentence is just? Do the victims of a war feel that the attack is just? Perhaps the only way to define justice is to say that an act is just only if all participants in the action feel that the act is just.
>
> Does justice only exist when all parties agree that a just act has occurred? Plan and write an essay in which you develop your point of view on this issue. Support your position with reasoning and examples taken from your reading, studies, experience, or observations.

_____

_____

_____

_____

_____

_____

_____

Now read over your paragraph. Look for the following:

1. Did you include a definitive thesis statement?

2. Did you elaborate on what your thesis means?

3. Did you list what examples you will use in your essay?

4. Did you avoid misspellings and grammatical errors?

BODY BUILDING

Now it's time to beef up your essay with some body paragraphs. Your essay should contain only two of them. Body paragraphs are where you develop your ideas by relating your examples to your thesis.

A good example should:

- Be specific rather than general

- Be explained in enough detail to make it clear to the reader how it supports your ideas

- Complement the other examples you mention and highlight a different side of your argument

- Always be explicitly tied back to your main idea

Try to start each body paragraph with a nice clear transition. It will help the flow of your essay. The following transitions are all useful:

However	Even though
While	Although
Moreover	In addition
Despite	

Each body paragraph should develop only one example. If you try to deal with more than one example, your essay will become muddled. Introduce your example and then demonstrate how your example supports your thesis. Remember our first prompt about blank slates and such? Here's a sample body paragraph on that topic:

An individual whose personality was not defined by the society around him was Gandhi. Gandhi was a product of a society that was dominated by imperialistic notions. The British Empire had India under its control. The powerful British navy and army were constant reminders of the military might of the British. Yet Gandhi was not a warlike person. Despite growing up in a violent society, Gandhi embraced peace. If Gandhi were truly a blank slate, it would stand to reason that he would adopt the combative personality of the institutions around him. Instead, his nonviolent ways show that there is more to personality than the effect of the society we are born into.

Your Turn—Exercise 10.2

Now it's your turn again. Using the prompt on justice, write a body paragraph.

_____

_____

_____

_____

_____

_____

_____

_____

_____

All done? Read over your paragraph and check for the following:

1. Does your paragraph begin with a transition?
2. Did you discuss only one example in the paragraph?
3. Did you relate your example back to your thesis, showing the reader how the example supports your point of view?
4. Did you have a minimum of spelling and grammar mistakes?

THAT'S A WRAP

The final thing your essay needs is a conclusion. Your conclusion doesn't have to be long, but make sure you wrap up your argument. Refer back to your examples and your original thesis. Sum up what you've said and answer the question, "Why do you see it this way?" Here is a sample conclusion:

There was much more to Nelson Mandela's and Gandhi's development than the influence of the society around them. There are many factors that shape a person's development and the fact that people can transcend the circumstances of their upbringings shows that some part of our personalities is inherent and ingrained.

Your Turn—Exercise 10.3

Guess what? It's your turn again. Write a conclusion paragraph to our prompt on justice.

_____

_____

_____

_____

_____

_____

_____

_____

_____

Now take a look at the finished product. Did you:

1. Sum up what you said in your thesis?
2. Refer back to your examples?
3. Avoid spelling and grammar mistakes?

TIME MANAGEMENT

One of the hardest things about the essay is balancing your time. You have 25 minutes to write, which is not a lot. Here's a rough guideline to help keep you on track:

- **First 3 minutes:** Think. Organize. Take a point of view. Brainstorm, and write down the examples you've picked.

- **Next 17–20 minutes:** Write. Try to balance your time between the intro and body paragraphs.

- **Last 2–5 minutes:** Conclusion. If you haven't done so already, begin writing your conclusion.

Take a breath. You're done!

One final consideration: Neatness does count. A legibly written essay makes your grader's job easier, and when your grader's job is easier, your grader is happy. And when your grader is happy, you will get a better score. So be as neat as possible. Indent your paragraphs. Use the margins of the page to align your essay. Avoid scratching out mistakes. Erase cleanly. All of these things can help the overall impression of your essay.

ESSAY SUMMARY

Keep the following in mind:

1. Your essay is graded holistically. The overall impression of the essay is what counts.

2. Give the essay grader what he or she wants. That means responding to the prompt, organizing your essay, and using examples.

3. Make sure your essay has an introduction, body paragraphs, and a conclusion.

4. Make sure you use examples to support your thesis.

5. A few grammatical and spelling errors are okay; one error every sentence is not.

It is not enough for a work of art to simply be beautiful. That is not the function of art. A true work of art should instruct and enlighten as well. It should speak to its viewer. It should give something to its audience. The true artists are the ones who convey messages or make statements with their art. Beauty alone is not a function or reason to exist.

Is there a place in this world for pure beauty or does an aesthetic piece need a functional aspect as well? Plan and write an essay in which you develop your point of view on this issue. Support your position with reasoning and examples taken from your reading, studies, experience, or observations.

_____

_____

_____

_____

_____

_____

_____

_____

_____

_____

_____

_____

_____

_____

_____

_____

_____

_____

_____

_____

_____

_____

_____

_____

_____

_____

_____

_____

_____

_____

_____

_____

_____

_____

_____

_____

_____

_____

_____

Vocab Time

Turn to pages 159–160 and memorize the Hit Parade Words for
Step 10.

THE PRINCETON REVIEW
HIT PARADE

The Hit Parade is a list of the most commonly tested words on the SAT. We can't guarantee that any of them will be on your SAT, but there's a good chance that there will be a few. Moreover, these words are typical of the kind of words that appear on the SAT. By learning these words, you'll be more alert to other words of the same type when you read a book or the newspaper.

Some people like using flash cards to learn vocabulary. If this works for you, do so. Another great way to learn words is to take a few words every day and use them at every opportunity. If, for instance, you're walking down the street with your friend and you come across a flower in a garden, say, "My, what an aesthetically pleasing plant." You will probably annoy your friends, but you will certainly learn these words.

In addition to learning these words, try to read as much as you can. While you're reading, note the words you don't know and look them up in a dictionary. For additional words, go to page 226.

STEP 1

clarity	clearness in thought or expression
cogent	convincing; reasonable
cohesive	condition of sticking together
compelling	forceful; urgently demanding attention
convoluted	intricate; complex
didactic	intended to instruct
dogmatic	characterized by a stubborn adherence to a belief
effusive	describing unrestrained emotional expression; pouring freely
emphatic	expressed or expressing with emphasis
florid	very flowery in style
fluid	easily flowing
hackneyed	overfamiliar through overuse; trite
rapport	a relationship of mutual trust or affinity
adage	a wise old saying
poignant	profoundly moving; touching
abstruse	hard to understand
arduous	difficult; strenuous
futile	serving no useful purpose
heinous	hatefully evil; abominable
impede	to slow the progress of; to interfere with
impenetrable	incapable of being penetrated; inaccessible

STEP 2

dilatory	tending to cause delay
enervate	to weaken the strength or vitality of
indolent	lazy
listless	lacking energy
sedentary	not migratory; involving much sitting; settled
soporific	causing sleep or sleepiness
stupor	a state of reduced or suspended sensibility
torpor	laziness; inactivity; dullness
paucity	an extreme lack of
ebullience	lively or enthusiastic expression
farce	a ridiculous or empty show
frenetic	frenzied or crazed
garrulous	given to excessive, rambling talk
gratuitous	given freely; unearned; unwarranted
insipid	uninteresting; unchallenging
ponderous	of great weight; dull
sonorous	having or producing sound; imposing or impressive
squalor	a filthy condition or quality
superfluous	extra; unnecessary
specious	having the ring of truth or plausibility but actually being false
slander	false charges and malicious oral statements or reports about someone
ruse	a crafty trick
egregious	conspicuously bad or offensive

facetious	playfully humorous
pander	to cater to the tastes and desires of others or exploit their weaknesses
propriety	appropriateness of behavior
wry	dryly humorous, often with a touch of irony
lampoon	(*n*) a broad satirical piece; (*v*) to broadly satire
parody	an artistic work that imitates the style of another work for comic effect

STEP 3

abdicate	to formally give up power
annihilate	to destroy completely
benevolent	kind; generous
despotic	characterized by exercising absolute power
dictatorial	domineering; oppressively overbearing
haughty	condescendingly proud
imperious	marked by arrogant assurance
omnipotent	all-powerful
patronizing	treating in a condescending manner
usurp	to take power by force
adamant	unyielding or inflexible
assiduous	hardworking
conscientious	careful and principled
diligent	marked by painstaking effort; hardworking
dogged	stubbornly persevering
exemplary	commendable; deserving imitation
fastidious	possessing careful attention to detail
intrepid	courageous; fearless

meticulous	extremely careful and precise
obstinate	stubbornly adhering to an opinion or a course of action
tenacity	persistent adherence to a belief or a point of view
milk	to draw or extract profit or advantage from
zealous	passionate; extremely interested in pursuing something
punctilious	strictly attentive to minute details; picky

STEP 4

alleviate	to ease a pain or a burden; to make more bearable
asylum	a place of retreat or security
auspicious	attended by favorable circumstances
benign	kind and gentle
emollient	softening and soothing
mitigate	to make less severe or painful
mollify	to calm or soothe
sanction	(v) to give official authorization or approval to
substantiated	supported with proof or evidence; verified
exculpate	to free from guilt or blame
debunk	to expose the falseness of
deleterious	having a harmful effect; injurious
disingenuous	not straightforward; crafty
disparate	fundamentally distinct or different
fabricated	made up; concocted in order to deceive
recalcitrant	defiant of authority; stubborn; not easily managed

spurious	not genuine; false
capricious	impulsive and unpredictable
disdain	feelings of contempt for others; to look down on others
glower	to look or stare angrily or sullenly
pejorative	describing words or phrases that belittle or speak negatively of someone
plagiarism	the act of passing off as one's own the ideas or writings of another
trite	unoriginal; overused; stale
vacuous	devoid of matter; empty
vilify	to lower in estimation or importance; to slander
disparage	to speak of in a slighting way or negatively; to belittle

STEP 5

aberration	a deviation from the way things normally happen or are done
dubious	doubtful; of doubtful outcome
ostentatious	describing a showy or pretentious display
quandary	a state of uncertainty or perplexity
stymied	thwarted; stumped; blocked
wily	cunning
aesthetic	having to do with beauty
decorous	proper; marked by good taste
embellish	to make beautiful by ornamenting; to add details to in order to make more attractive
idyllic	simple and carefree
medley	an assortment or a mixture, especially of musical pieces

mural	a big painting applied directly to a wall
opulent	exhibiting a display of great wealth
ornate	elaborately ornamented
pristine	not spoiled; pure
serene	calm
lucid	clear to the understanding; sane
affable	easygoing; friendly
amenable	responsive; agreeable
amiable	good-natured and likable
camaraderie	goodwill between friends
cordial	warm and sincere; friendly
gregarious	enjoying the company of others; sociable; outgoing
salutary	promoting good health
sanguine	cheerfully confident; optimistic
innocuous	having no bad effect; harmless

STEP 6

brusque	describing a rudely abrupt manner
cantankerous	grumpy; disagreeable
caustic	bitingly sarcastic or witty
contemptuous	feeling hatred; scornful; despising
feral	savage, fierce, or untamed
fractious	quarrelsome; unruly
incorrigible	unable to be reformed
ingrate	an ungrateful person
insolent	insulting in manner or speech; rude

malevolent	having or exhibiting ill will; wishing harm to others; hateful; evil
notorious	known widely and unfavorably; infamous
obdurate	stubborn; inflexible; stubbornly persisting in wrongdoing
repugnant	causing disgust or hatred
unpalatable	not pleasing to the taste
parsimonious	frugal to the point of stinginess
itinerant	traveling from place to place
remote	located far away; secluded
transitory	short-lived or temporary
unfettered	free from restrictions or bonds
harbinger	one that indicates what is to come; a forerunner
ominous	menacing; threatening
portend	to serve as an omen or a warning of
prophetic	foretelling or predicting future events
impromptu	not planned in advance; spur of the moment

STEP 7

ambiguous	open to more than one interpretation; not clear
ambivalent	simultaneously feeling opposing feelings, such as love and hate
arbiter	a judge who decides a disputed issue
inconsequential	unimportant
ample	describing an adequate or more-than-adequate amount of something
burgeoning	expanding or growing
capacious	roomy; spacious

copious	plentiful; large in quantity
permeate	spread throughout; to pass through the pores of
prodigious	enormous; exciting amazement or wonder
replete	abundantly supplied; filled
candor	sincerity; openness; frankness
frank	open and sincere in expression; straightforward; candid
pragmatic	practical
purist	one who is particularly concerned with maintaining traditional practices
terse	brief and to the point; concise
insightful	perceptive
curtailed	cut short; abbreviated
arid	describing a dry, rainless climate
conflagration	a widespread fire
nocturnal	of or occurring in the night
temperate	moderate; mild

STEP 8

clandestine	secretive, especially in regards to concealing an illicit purpose
coup	a brilliant and sudden overthrow of a government
enmity	mutual hatred or ill will
heresy	an opinion that disagrees with established, dearly held beliefs
implacable	impossible to appease or satisfy
maverick	one who is independent and resists adherence to a group

mercurial	quick and changeable in mood
pugnacious	combative; belligerent; quarrelsome
rancorous	hateful; marked by deep seated ill will
stratagem	a clever trick used to deceive or outwit
wary	on guard; watchful
thwart	to prevent the occurrence of; to successfully oppose
reclamation	a restoration or rehabilitation to productivity or usefulness; the process of reclaiming
furtive	characterized by stealth; sneaky
impetuous	characterized by sudden energy or emotion; impulsive
catalog	(*v*) to make an itemized list of
equanimity	the quality of being calm and even-tempered; composure
feasible	capable of being accomplished; possible
apt	suitable; appropriate
solvent	able to pay one's debts
facile	done or achieved with little effort; easy
liquid	flowing readily
plausible	seemingly valid or acceptable; credible; believable
biased	prejudiced
incontrovertible	indisputable; not open to question
jurisprudence	the philosophy or science of law
vindicated	freed from blame
penitent	expressing remorse for one's misdeeds

STEP 9

incumbent	(*adj*) imposed as a duty; obligatory
indigenous	originating and living in a particular area
innate	possessed at birth; inborn
inveterate	long established; deep-rooted; habitual
parochial	narrow in scope; of or relating to a church parish
pervasive	having the quality or tendency to be everywhere at the same time
impinge	to have an effect or make an impression
laconic	using few words; concise
lament	to express grief for; mourn
obsolete	no longer in use; old-fashioned
reticent	reluctant to speak
sanction	(*n*) an economic or military measure put in place to punish another country
suppressed	subdued; kept from being circulated
surreptitious	done by secretive means
truncated	shortened; cut off
wane	to decrease gradually in intensity; decline
ephemeral	lasting for a markedly brief time; fleeting
obscure	(*adj*) relatively unknown; (*v*) to conceal or make indistinct
tacit	implied but not actually expressed
tenuous	having little substance or strength; shaky; flimsy
timorous	shy; timid
trepidation	uncertainty; apprehension
immutable	not able to be changed

mundane	commonplace; ordinary
prosaic	unimaginative; dull

STEP 10

prudent	exercising good judgment or common sense
tenet	a principle held as being true by a person or an organization
stoic	indifferent to pleasure or pain; impassive
austere	somber, stern, unadorned, and simple
genre	describing a category of artistic endeavor; characterized by style, content, or form
staid	characterized by a straitlaced sense of propriety; serious
archaic	characteristic of an earlier, more primitive period; old-fashioned
emulate	to try to equal through imitation
naïve	lacking sophistication
nascent	coming into existence; emerging
novice	a beginner
toxic	poisonous
brittle	easily broken, cracked, or snapped when subjected to pressure
malice	extreme ill will or spite
malfeasance	misconduct or wrongdoing, especially by a public official
dilettante	a dabbler; one who superficially understands an art or a field of knowledge
eclectic	made up of a variety of sources or styles

intuitive	known or perceived by intuition
laudatory	expressing great praise
novel	strikingly new, unusual, or different
paramount	supreme; dominant; superior to all others
urbane	notably polite and elegant in manner; suave
epiphany	a sudden burst of understanding or discovery
trenchant	keen; incisive
whimsical	subject to erratic behavior; unpredictable; acting on a whim

PART II

PRACTICE PROBLEMS
WITH EXPLANATIONS

The following drills will allow you to reinforce and refine the techniques you have learned in this book. If you have the time, we highly recommend that you take a few SATs under timed conditions. This will give you the best possible practice, and help you prepare yourself mentally and physically for the actual test. A good book of such tests is *11 Practice Tests for the SAT & PSAT*. You can find it at any large bookstore or online and at www.PrincetonReview.com.

DEFINITIONS

2. Which of the following is equal to the product of two consecutive integers?

    (A) 55
    (B) 56
    (C) 57
    (D) 58
    (E) 59

3. If $y \neq 0$, then $(y^3)^2 \div y^2 =$

    (A) 1
    (B) y^2
    (C) y^3
    (D) y^4
    (E) y^6

5. A rectangle with length 10 and width 4 has an area that is twice the area of a triangle with base 2. What is the height of the triangle?

    (A) 10
    (B) 15
    (C) 20
    (D) 30
    (E) 40

6. If $s = 4$, then $2s^2 + (2s)^2 =$

    (A) 32
    (B) 64
    (C) 96
    (D) 108
    (E) 128

2. **B**   To get a product of about 50, the two consecutive numbers would need to be between 6 and 9. Try some consecutive integers and see what you get. $6 \times 7 = 42$, which is too small. $7 \times 8 = 56$, which is choice B.

3. **D** $(y^3)^2$ is the same thing as y^6, so the original equation $(y^3)^2 \div y^2$ is the same thing as $\frac{y^6}{y^2}$, which reduces to y^4. Therefore the answer is D.

5. **C**   The area of the rectangle is $b \times h$, so its area is $10 \times 4 = 40$. If the area of the triangle is half of 40, this means that $\frac{1}{2}(b \times h) = 20$. You know that the base is 2, so we can solve for h, which must equal 20. Therefore the answer is C.

6. **C**   If you substitute 4 for s, the equation reads $2(4)^2 + (2 \times 4)^2$. Multiply this out, and you get $32 + 64$, which is 96—choice C.

11. 60% of 80 is the same as 40% of what number?

(A) 100
(B) 105
(C) 110
(D) 120
(E) 140

13. If r is a prime number greater than 2, which of the following is NOT a factor of $4r$?

(A) r
(B) r^2
(C) $2r$
(D) $4r$
(E) 4

14. If the average of x, y, and z is 28 and the average of x and y is 12, what is the value of z ?

(A) 14
(B) 28
(C) 42
(D) 60
(E) 84

11. **D** 60% of 80 translates to $\frac{60}{100} \times 80$, which is the same as 48. So the problem now reads: 48 is the same as 40% of what number? You can translate this question to $48 = \frac{40}{100} x$. Then, you can solve for x, which equals 120; choice D.

13. **B** Probably the best way to approach this question is by Plugging In. Pick a prime number greater than 2 to be the value of r. Use $r = 3$. Using this number for r, the question becomes: Which of the following is NOT a factor of 12? Answer choices A through E become 3, 9, 6, 12, and 4, respectively. Which is not a factor of 12? Choice B.

14. **D** Because average $= \frac{total}{number}$ and the average of x, y, and z is 28, you know that $28 = \frac{x+y+z}{3}$. You don't know what x, y, and z are individually, but you know that $x + y + z = 84$. Likewise, because the average of x and y is 12, you know that $x + y = 24$. The value of z must be the difference between 84 and 24, or 60. The correct answer is D.

PLUGGING IN

4. What is the least of four consecutive
   integers whose sum is 22?

   (A) 3
   (B) 4
   (C) 5
   (D) 6
   (E) 7

8. If $3^{x+2} = 81$, what is the value of x ?

   (A) 1
   (B) 2
   (C) 3
   (D) 4
   (E) 5

14. The width of a rectangle is twice its
    height. If the perimeter of the rectangle is
    48, what is its height?

   (A) 8
   (B) 10
   (C) 12
   (D) 18
   (E) 24

4. **B**   Begin by Plugging In the middle answer choice, 5. If 5 is the least of four consecutive integers, the integers would be 5, 6, 7, and 8. The sum of these numbers is 26, which is too large. So try choice B. If 4 is the least of the numbers, the numbers would be 4, 5, 6, and 7. The sum of these number is 22. So the answer is B.

8. **B**   Start with the middle choice, and assume that x is 3. Is $3^5 = 81$? No, it's larger than 81. So try choice B, and Plug In 2 for x. Is $3^4 = 81$? Yes. So the answer is B.

14. **A**   Start with choice C and Plug In 12 for the height of the rectangle. If the width of the rectangle is twice the height, then the width must be 24. The perimeter will be 12 + 24 + 12 + 24, or 72. Choice C is not right. Try choice B, and Plug In 10 for the height. If the height is 10, the width must be 20, and the perimeter becomes 10 + 20 + 10 + 20, or 60. This result is still too big. So the answer must be A. Try it to be sure. If the height is 8, the width is 16, and the perimeter is 8 + 16 + 8 + 16, which is 48.

15. John and Tim together weigh 230 pounds. If John's weight is 20 pounds more than twice Tim's weight, what is Tim's weight in pounds?

(A) 40

(B) 50

(C) 60

(D) 70

(E) 80

16. What is the lowest possible integer for which 30 percent of that integer is greater than 1.5?

(A) 2

(B) 3

(C) 5

(D) 6

(E) 7

17. The sum of the integers r and s is 186. The units digit of r is 5. If r is divided by 5, the result is equal to s. What is the value of r ?

(A) 55

(B) 60

(C) 90

(D) 95

(E) 155

15. **D**   Begin by Plugging In choice C, or 60, for Tim's weight. If John weighs 20 pounds more than twice Tim's weight, John must weigh 20 + 2(60) = 140, and together they would weigh 200 pounds. But you know that together they should weigh 230 pounds. So C is too small. Try choice D. If Tim weighs 70 pounds, then John would weigh 20 + 2(70) = 160 pounds. And, indeed, John and Tim together would weigh 230 pounds. So the answer is D.

16. **D**   Start with choice C. Is 30% of 5 greater than 1.5? $\dfrac{30}{100} \times 5$ is equal to 1.5, but not greater than 1.5; therefore, C is too small; the answer must be D.

17. **E**   In this case, don't forget to use common sense: The problem says that the units digit of r is 5, so choices B and C can be eliminated right away. Try choice D, and Plug In 95 for r. The problem states that s is equal to r divided by 5. Because you're Plugging In 95 for r, that means that $s = 19$, and that $r + s = 114$. But $r + s$ should equal 186. So D is too small. Try E. When we Plug In 155 for r, s becomes 31. Is 155 + 31 = 186? Yes, and the answer is E.

PLUGGING IN YOUR OWN NUMBERS

5. If x is an odd integer greater than 1, what is the next greater odd integer in terms of x ?

(A) $x + 1$

(B) $x + 2$

(C) $x - 2$

(D) $2x + 1$

(E) $2x - 1$

6. If $t \neq 0$, then $\dfrac{\frac{1}{8}}{2t} =$

(A) $\dfrac{1}{8}t$

(B) $\dfrac{4}{t}$

(C) $\dfrac{t}{4}$

(D) $2t$

(E) $4t$

7. The cost of four shirts is d dollars. At this rate, what is the cost, in cents, of 16 shirts?

(A) $4d$

(B) $16d$

(C) $\dfrac{100d}{16}$

(D) $400d$

(E) $1,600d$

5. **B**   Plug In 3 for x. Now the question reads: What is the next greater odd integer? It's 5. Which choice says 5? B does.

6. **C**   Plug In 2 for t. Now the problem reads: $\dfrac{\frac{1}{8}}{2(2)}$ which is the same as $\dfrac{\frac{1}{8}}{4}$ or $\dfrac{1}{2}$. Which choice says $\dfrac{1}{2}$? C does.

7. **D**   Plug In a nice round number like 5 for d. If four shirts cost 5 dollars, then 16 shirts cost 20 dollars. But the problem asks for the answer in cents. 20 dollars is the same as 2,000 cents. Which choice says 2,000 when you Plug In your numbers? D does.

13. If a is b more than three times c, what is b in terms of a and c ?

(A) $a + \dfrac{1}{3}c$

(B) $a + 3c$

(C) $a - \dfrac{1}{3}c$

(D) $a - 3c$

(E) $\dfrac{a - c}{2}$

16. If the sum of three consecutive integers is y, then, in terms of y, what is the least of these integers?

(A) $\dfrac{y}{3}$

(B) $\dfrac{y - 1}{3}$

(C) $\dfrac{y - 2}{3}$

(D) $\dfrac{y - 3}{3}$

(E) $\dfrac{y - 4}{3}$

20. If x is an odd integer and $4^x = y$, which of the following equals $16y$ in terms of x ?

(A) 4^x

(B) $4^{x + 2}$

(C) 4^{2x}

(D) $4x^2$

(E) 16^x

13. **D**   Plug In numbers for a, b, and c that obey the rule in the problem that $a = b + 3(c)$. How about 19, 4, and 5 for a, b, and c, respectively. This obeys the rule, because $19 = 4 + 3(5)$. Now the question asks "What is b?" The answer is 4. Which choice says 4? D does.

16. **D**   Plug In a number for y that's the sum of three consecutive integers. Because $4 + 5 + 6 = 15$, you can pick 15 for y. Now the question asks: What is the least of these integers? Plugging In your numbers, the answer is 4. Which of the choices says 4? D does.

20. **B**   Plug In some numbers for x and y that obey the rule that $4^x = y$. One set you could pick would be 3 and 64, because $4^3 = 64$. Now the question asks: Which of the following equals $16y$? Because our y is 64, the question asks: Which of the following is equal to 16×64, or 1,024? Which choice equals 1,024? B does.

GEOMETRY

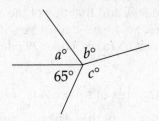

3. In the figure above, what is the value of $a + b + c$?

   (A) 115
   (B) 125
   (C) 235
   (D) 295
   (E) 305

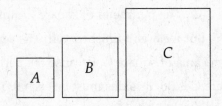

9. In the figure above, the perimeter of square A is $\frac{2}{3}$ the perimeter of square B, and the perimeter of square B is $\frac{2}{3}$ the perimeter of square C. If the area of square A is 16, what is the area of square C ?

   (A) 24
   (B) 36
   (C) 64
   (D) 72
   (E) 81

3. **D**   In this case, all you know is that the degrees must add up to 360, and that one of the angles measures 65 degrees. So $a + b + c$ must be whatever is left when you subtract 65 from 360, or 295 degrees. The answer is D.

9. **E**   Because the area of square A is 16, you know that its sides all have length 4. The perimeter of square A is therefore also 16. We know that the perimeter of square A is $\frac{2}{3}$ the perimeter of square B, so we can calculate the perimeter of square B to be $16 = \frac{2}{3}$ B. The perimeter of square B must therefore be 24. Likewise, the perimeter of square B is $\frac{2}{3}$ the perimeter of square C, so you can calculate the perimeter of square C by $24 = \frac{2}{3}$ C. The perimeter of square C must therefore be 36. But we aren't finished yet! The problem asks for the area of square C. Because the perimeter of square C is 36, its sides must be each 9. The area of square C is therefore $9 \times 9 = 81$. The answer is E.

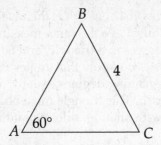

B

4

60°

A   C

Note: Figure not drawn to scale

11. In the figure above, if $\overline{AB} = \overline{AC}$, then $\overline{AB} =$

(A) 2

(B) 4

(C) $2\sqrt{2}$

(D) $2\sqrt{3}$

(E) $4\sqrt{3}$

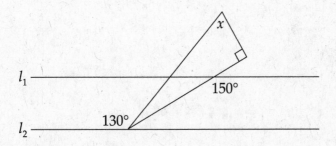

13. If l_1 is parallel to l_2 in the figure above, what is the value of x ?

(A) 20

(B) 50

(C) 70

(D) 80

(E) 90

11. **B** If you know that $\overline{AB} = \overline{AC}$, then we know that angles B and C must have the same measure. Because there are 180 degrees in a triangle, and 60 of them make up angle A, you know that angles B and C must split the 120 remaining degrees equally, and measure 60 degrees each. This triangle must be an equilateral triangle, with all of its sides equal to 4. The answer is B.

13. **C** Don't forget to use POE! We know that x could not be as small as 20 degrees or as big as 90 degrees, so you can eliminate choices A and E. Because l_1 is parallel to l_2, you know that 130 degrees plus the other angle in the triangle must equal 150 degrees. You can determine that the bottom angle is 20 degrees, which means that x is 70 degrees.

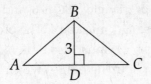

12. The area of triangle *DBC* is 6. If $\overline{AD} =$ $\overline{DC}$, what is the area of triangle *ABC* ?

(A) 4
(B) 6
(C) 12
(D) 18
(E) 24

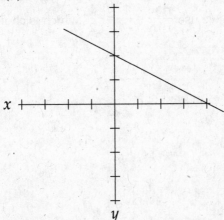

15. What is the slope of the line shown in the figure above?

(A) –2
(B) $-\dfrac{1}{2}$
(C) 0
(D) $\dfrac{1}{2}$
(E) 2

12. **C**   If the area of triangle *DBC* is 6, and its height is 3, then its base $\overline{DC}$ must be 4. The problem says that $\overline{AD} = \overline{DC}$, so $\overline{AD}$ must also be 4. Now you can solve for the area of triangle *ABC*, which has a base of 8 and a height of 3. The answer is C.

15. **B**   Don't forget to eliminate first! The line must have a negative slope, so you can eliminate choices C, D, and E. If nothing else, you have a 50 percent chance of a correct answer. The two points at which the line touches the axes are at (4,0) and (0,2). To calculate slope, we use $\dfrac{\text{rise}}{\text{run}} = \dfrac{2}{-4} = -\dfrac{1}{2}$, which is choice B.

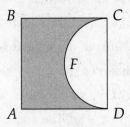

16. If *ABCD* is a square and *CFD* is a semi-circular arc with radius 4, what is the area of the shaded region?

(A) $16 - 8\pi$

(B) $16 - 8\pi$

(C) $64 - 8\pi$

(D) $64 - 16\pi$

(E) 64

16. **C**   If the radius of the semicircle is 4, then the side of the square must be 8, and the square has an area of 64. 64 minus the area of the semicircle will give us the area of the shaded region. The area of the semicircle is half the area of the whole circle, which has radius 4, or $\frac{1}{2}\pi(4)^2$, which is 8π. The area of the shaded region is therefore $64 - 8\pi$, or choice C.

SENTENCE COMPLETIONS

1. Although he is usually very _____ at such occasions, John was surprisingly quiet at his engagement party.

   (A) reserved
   (B) outgoing
   (C) successful
   (D) irreverent
   (E) vague

2. Although a certain number of people loved Isabel's new play, it never achieved the _____ success necessary for a long run in theaters.

   (A) intellectual
   (B) eccentric
   (C) persuasive
   (D) dignified
   (E) popular

3. Unfortunately, many of Aristotle's works are _____ to us, because they were _____ along with the ancient library at Alexandria. .

   (A) unknown . . promoted
   (B) lost . . destroyed
   (C) meaningless . . investigated
   (D) important . . chastised
   (E) clear . . suppressed

1. **B**   The trigger word "though" combined with the clue "surprisingly quiet" tells us that the word in the blank must be a word that means the opposite of *quiet*. The best choice is B.

2. **E**   The trigger word "although" combined with "a certain number of people loved Isabel's play" tells us that there were not enough people who loved her play to make it a success. The word in the blank must be a word that means *widespread*. The best choice is E.

3. **B**   Solve this problem one blank at a time. The word "unfortunately" tells us that the word in the first blank must have a negative connotation such as *lost*. This will eliminate choices D and E, but at this point, A, B, and C are still possible. Now look at the second blank. The second blank must contain a word like "ruined." Of the choices that are left, B is the best.

4. The team captain is an extremely
_____ man; he inevitably tries to take all
the credit for his team's victories.

(A) composed

(B) plentiful

(C) egoistic

(D) cooperative

(E) articulate

5. The _____ water made it extremely
difficult for the divers to search for the
sunken treasure.

(A) transparent

(B) malodorous

(C) hazardous

(D) turbulent

(E) sparkling

6. Despite early election results that
predicted his defeat, Senator Thomas
remained _____ that he would win
the day.

(A) doubtful

(B) ignorant

(C) amicable

(D) philanthropic

(E) confident

4. **C**   The clue in this sentence is "he inevitably tries to take all the credit for his team's victories." The word in the blank must be a word that describes such a person. The best choice is therefore C.

5. **D**   The clue in this sentence is "made it extremely difficult for the divers to search." What might describe water that makes it difficult to search? Perhaps a word like "murky" or "choppy." The only choice that comes close is choice D.

6. **E**   The trigger word "despite" combined with the clue "early election results that predicted his defeat" means that the word in the blank must be a word like "certain" or "convinced." The only close choice is E.

7. Despite their very _____ cultural and religious backgrounds, the leaders of the civil rights march were able to put their differences behind them and fight for a _____ goal.

   (A) diverse . . common
   (B) different . . poetic
   (C) similar . . joint
   (D) indifferent . . impossible
   (E) incompatible . . remote

8. Unlike her father, who never missed an opportunity to praise the works of Charles Dickens, Amy thought that *A Tale of Two Cities* was _____.

   (A) excessive
   (B) mediocre
   (C) ingenious
   (D) ambiguous
   (E) anecdotal

9. The company president was not a very _____ person; he would constantly dream up projects that were impossible to carry out.

   (A) radical
   (B) pragmatic
   (C) meticulous
   (D) suspenseful
   (E) inflammatory

10. She was a very _____ student; she checked every reference in her papers and always used the correct form in her footnotes.

    (A) prodigious
    (B) supercilious
    (C) punctilious
    (D) acute
    (E) inspirational

7. **A**   Start with the second blank. The clue for the second blank is "were able to put their differences behind them." What kind of word might describe such a goal? A word that means *cooperative* or *combined*. So you can eliminate B, D, and E. Now look at the first blank. The trigger word "despite" means that the word in the blank must be the opposite of *cooperative* or *combined*. The best answer is A.

8. **B**   The clue in this sentence is "Unlike her father, who never missed an opportunity to praise." So you know that Amy does not like Dickens. Even if you can't think of your own word for the blank, you know it must be a negative word, so you can eliminate C, D, and E and you have at least a 50 percent chance of picking the correct answer. The best answer (and the most negative of the five choices) is B.

9. **B**   The clue in this sentence is "would constantly dream up projects that were impossible to carry out." Such a person is not very realistic or practical. The best answer is B.

10. **C**   The clue in this sentence is "she checked every reference in her papers and always used the correct form in her footnotes." What kind of word describes such a person? Careful, or a good worker. The choices in this question are all hard words, but by elimination you should be able to take a good guess. The best answer is C.

ERROR IDENTIFICATION

1. In 1976, to celebrate the Bicentennial

    of the United States, classes from each

    local school <u>attended</u> a grand fireworks
                    A

    display and, <u>having</u> never seen such a
                    B

    display before, <u>was surprised</u> by the
                         C

    colors and the noise <u>caused by</u> the con-
                             D

    trolled explosions. <u>No error</u>
                           E

2. The only people foolish <u>enough</u> <u>to enter</u>
                               A   B

    the haunted mansion <u>on Halloween</u> are
                            C

    <u>us</u>. <u>No error</u>
    D   E

3. <u>Considering</u> the blinding snowstorm
       A

    <u>and</u> ice-covered roads, you and <u>her</u> were
    B   C

    lucky <u>to arrive</u> here safely. <u>No error</u>
             D   E

4. <u>Be sure</u> to take the proofs over to Kim or
       A

    <u>I</u> in the production room <u>when</u> you
    B   C

    <u>have finished</u> the layout. <u>No error</u>
       D   E

1. **C**   The verb "was surprised" is singular, but the subject is "classes," which is plural.

2. **D**   This question contains a pronoun case error. The tough question here is whether the word "us" is a subject (that does the action) or an object (that receives the action). The sentence is confusing because it inverts the normal sentence structure and the subject is the last word. We can see this if we rewrite the sentence in the traditional structure, "we are the only people foolish enough…," therefore "us" is meant to be a subject and the pronoun "we" is needed.

3. **C**   This sentence contains a pronoun case error. The use of the pronoun "her" is incorrect because it is the subject of the sentence and "her" is an object pronoun. A good way to see this error is to remove the other subject noun, you, and read the sentence again. The correct word is the subject pronoun "she."

4. **B**   The issue here is pronoun case. A good way to see this error is to remove the other object noun, Kim, and read the sentence again. The correct pronoun is "me."

5. Running 20 miles is much more difficult than
   A   B

    to walk the same distance because of the
                                   C

    stress that running puts on an athlete's joints.
                     D

    No error
       E

6. Although celebrities and fans need each other
       A   B

    to maintain our culture's obsession with
          C

    fame, they can develop resentment about the
              D

    demands placed upon them.

    No error
       E

7. After seeking advice from the council, the
       A   B   C

    brave hero rode to the mountaintop to slay the

    dragon plaguing the village. No error
               D   E

8. The teacher noted that the inspired writing
                A

    Joe displayed on his homework was
                  B

    incompatible to the prosaic prose he produced
          C   D

    in class. No error
             E

5. **A**   This sentence incorrectly compares "running" to "to walk." To be parallel, the sentence should read "To run . . . is . . . to walk . . ."

6. **D**   This is a pronoun ambiguity question because "they" could refer to celebrities or fans.

7. **E**   This sentence is correct as written.

8. **C**   Always check prepositions (little words that show place) for idioms. The correct idiom is "incompatible with."

IMPROVING SENTENCES

9. In the summer, the Ruddy Duck <u>male,</u>
   <u>who lives in marshes, have</u> chestnut
   colored plumage and its bill is blue, but
   in the winter, the male is brown with a
   creamy colored face.

   (A) male, who lives in marshes, have
   (B) male was living in marshes and has
   (C) male that lives in marshes, it has
   (D) male lives in marshes with its
   (E) male, which lives in marshes, has

10. A dog that approaches a human slowly,
    looking into his eyes, walking as if on tip-
    toe, ears up, tail up and wagging slowly,
    <u>are likely indicators</u> that it may bite if it
    feels threatened.

    (A) are likely indicators
    (B) is likely an indicator
    (C) are likely indicating
    (D) is likely indicating
    (E) is likely an indication

9. **E**   Choice A incorrectly uses "who" to refer to an animal and contains a subject-verb error. B creates a run-on and incorrectly introduces the past tense into the sentence. C contains a comma splice and changes the meaning of the sentence by suggesting that the description applies only to Ruddy Duck males that live in the marshes. D adds an unnecessary verb into the main part of the sentence and creates a run-on.

10. **D**   Choices A and C incorrectly use a plural verb with the singular subject "a dog"; choices B and E incorrectly imply that the dog itself is an indication rather than that the dog may be indicating something by its actions.

11. Today's progressive companies are looking to recruit job candidates who <u>are educated, outgoing, and with proven track records within their industries,</u> decreasing the need to spend valuable company dollars on training.

(A) are educated, outgoing, and with proven track records within their industries,

(B) are educated, outgoing, and have proven track records within their industries,

(C) have higher degrees of education, outgoing qualities, and proven track records within their industries,

(D) have higher degrees of education, have outgoing qualities, and have proven track records within their industries,

(E) are educated, are outgoing, and who have proven track records within their industries,

12. Jason, who was the Vice President of Sales at ABC Book Company, found his high-paying job very boring, <u>as opposed to William's job as editor</u>.

(A) as opposed to William's job as editor

(B) as opposed to William's

(C) as opposed to William

(D) unlike what William did

(E) unlike William

11. **C**   Choice C is correct because it maintains parallel structure. Choices A, B, and E mix verbs and are not parallel in structure. Although choice D is parallel in structure, the verb "have" is repeated three times, making choice C the better choice.

12. **A**   The sentence is correct as written because it compares Jason's job to William's job. Choice B is incorrect because it is not known what "William's" is referring to. Choices C and E can be eliminated as they both compare Jason's job to William.

IMPROVING PARAGRAPHS

(1) *Snow is a major problem during winter.* (2) *Plenty of kids enjoy sledding and building snowmen; snow also makes beautiful scenery.* (3) *Although it is pretty and fun, it must be removed so our society can function even though it is entertaining.* (4) *There are pros and cons to every type of snow removal so it is hard to pick the best.*

(5) *Salt is useful and helpful when snow isn't too deep.* (6) *It melts snow quickly.* (7) *However, the problem with salt is that it is only workable on a small scale.* (8) *It's too expensive and timely to cover all the streets in a city.*

(9) *Plowing is another tool and it moves snow quickly.* (10) *Plowing is better if a city has many streets and a lot of snow.* (11) *However, plows rip up the road with their plows causing potholes and they don't eliminate snow they just move it.* (12) *So it's hard to pull your car out if you're parallel parked.*

(13) *Salting and plowing are both useful to an extent in their own ways, but salting and plowing also have significant disadvantages.* (14) *Society must invent a better way to remove snow so society can function well.*

13. Which of the following is the best version of sentence 3 (reproduced below)?

    Although it is pretty and fun, it must be removed so our society can function even though it is entertaining.

    (A) (As it is now.)
    (B) Although it is lovely and entertaining, snow must be removed so our society can function.
    (C) Functioning society commands the removal of pretty, fun snow so that it can function.
    (D) Removing entertaining snow ensures a functioning society.
    (E) Pretty and fun snow is entertaining and must be removed so our society can function.

13. **B**   Choice B is correct because it is the smoothest and least repetitive sentence. E could work if the conjunction "and" were "but." C has a redundancy problem. D promises something more than the original sentence does, as it seems to say that all society needs to function properly is snow removal. A is repetitive.

14. Which of the following is the best replace-
ment for the underlined word in sentence
8 (reproduced below)?

*It's too expensive and <u>timely</u> to cover all
the streets in a city.*

(A) Efficient
(B) Functioning
(C) Rapid
(D) Time-consuming
(E) Classic

15. Which of the following changes would
most improve sentence 10 (reproduced
below)?

*Plowing is better if a city has many streets
and a lot of snow.*

(A) Provide more circumstances in which
plowing is better.
(B) Divide sentence 10 into two sentences.
(C) Describe why plowing is better if
there are many streets and a lot of
snow.
(D) Insert a comma after "better."
(E) Remove "and a lot of snow."

14. **D**   "Timely" means efficient. The author misuses this word in the sentence. Instead, the sentence calls for a negative word given the first words: "It's too expensive to cover." If salt were efficient, it would be able to "cover" the streets. Therefore, A, B, and C are incorrect. E is not relevant to the sentence. D is the best choice because it shows why the salt could not "cover" the streets.

15. **C**   Choice B is incorrect because the sentence is not a run-on. D adds poor punctuation. E removes a relevant portion of the sentence. Choice A would add to the sentence, but C adds more because a reason is needed here for plowing's superiority.

16. Which of the following is the best version of sentence 11 (reproduced below)?

However, plows rip up the road with their plows causing potholes and they don't eliminate snow they just move it.

(A) Causing potholes, the road is ripped up by plows and don't eliminate snow, but move it.

(B) Plows cause potholes and move snow.

(C) Plows cause rips in the road called potholes, instead of eliminating snow, they move it.

(D) However, instead of eliminating snow, plows move it and cause rips in the road called potholes.

(E) However, plows rip potholes in the road moving the snow. They also move snow rather than eliminate it.

17. Which of the following would be the most appropriate title for this essay?

(A) The Problems with Different Types of Snow Removal

(B) Advantages and Disadvantages of Snow Removal Methods

(C) The Pleasures of Snow Removal

(D) Winter Issues of Society

(E) Driving through Snowy Streets

16. **D**   Choice A contains a number of modifier and subject errors. B is too simplistic and leaves out too much of the original sentence. C has a sentence splice comma error. E contains redundancies. D is the best in terms of clarity, correct grammar, and structure.

17. **B**   Choice C is nonexistent in the essay. Choices D and E are mentioned only briefly, not enough to justify a title. A is possible because much of the essay does discuss the problems. B is the best answer because it discusses both the advantages and the disadvantages.

CRITICAL READING

Questions 1–2 are based on the following passage.

Competing in the America's Cup—one of the world's premier sailing events—is considered the pinnacle of one's
career for sailors of expensive racing yachts. Rather than
Line allowing retired boats to sit idle, two yacht-racing enthu-
5 siasts created a new competition. Racing boats that have
won or raced in previous America's Cup competitions
will now have a chance to compete in a series of four
regattas across San Francisco Bay, thereby allowing their
owners to keep history alive. Restoring older vessels may
10 be costly, but it will ensure that legendary yachts, like the
champion *Stars & Stripes*, are maintained and enjoyed
past their prime.

1. As used in the context of the first sentence, "premier" most nearly means

   (A) first performance
   (B) foremost
   (C) high cost
   (D) foreign
   (E) preferred type

2. It can be inferred from the passage that

   (A) the *Stars & Stripes* will likely race in
   the newly created competition
   (B) retired yachts can race only in this
   new competition
   (C) restoring retired yachts is more
   expensive than building new ones
   (D) the America's Cup takes place in the
   San Francisco Bay area
   (E) yachts need restoration due to
   competing in the America's Cup

1. **B** The America's Cup is one of the leading sailing competitions. Choices A and C are valid definitions of "premier" but not appropriate in this context. Choices D and E are not valid definitions in any context.

2. **A** The *Stars & Stripes* is mentioned as one of the champion boats that will be "maintained and enjoyed past their prime." The word "only" in choice B is too extreme. C is incorrect because the cost of building a new yacht is not mentioned in the passage. Eliminate D because the passage doesn't state where the America's Cup takes place, just that the new competition will take place in San Francisco. E is an incorrect reading of the passage.

Questions 3–4 are based on the following passage.

The identity of the mysterious woman in Mr. Rochester's
attic in Charlotte Brontë's *Jane Eyre* is always a stunning
revelation for the first time reader. Many critics argue that
Line the significance of an insane first wife is more than just a
5 plot twist, however. Instead, they suggest that Bertha Mason,
the madwoman locked in the attic, can be read as a foil for
Jane herself. Trapped in the attic, raving and ignored, Bertha
represents the anger of all women in Victorian culture,
ensnared in a patriarchal system that denied them rights and
10 freedom. Through displacing what would be Jane's anger
onto this figure, Brontë allows for these emotions to be
expressed without overwhelming the book's main character
and narrative.

3. The introduction of the critics' argument
   serves to

   (A) explain why *Jane Eyre* is seen as such a
       significant novel

   (B) shift the attention from Jane Eyre to
       Bertha Mason

   (C) emphasize the surprise experienced by all
       readers

   (D) shift the focus from the specific to the
       universal

   (E) shift the argument from the grounds of
       reaction to analysis

3. **E**   The passage moves from how the first time reader feels to how critics interpret the meaning of the narrative. Choice A is not the credited answer because the passage is not concerned with explaining the novel's significance. B is not correct because the passage is concerned with Bertha Mason's relation to Jane Eyre, not Bertha Mason in and of herself. The critics' argument is meant to show that the identity is "more than just a plot twist, however," so choice C is not the credited answer. Choice D is too broad; the passage moves to thinking about connections with broader Victorian contexts, but not universal ideas.

4. According to the passage, in literary terms, Bertha Mason serves as Jane Eyre's

   (A) archetype, in that she precedes Jane in the text

   (B) doppelganger, or evil double, in that she mirrors Jane's dark side

   (C) anti-hero, in that she represents a satirical hero figure

   (D) antagonist, in that the plot deals with her opposition to Jane

   (E) protagonist, in that she is the primary figure in the text

4. **B**   A doppelganger, which we can tell from the rest of the answer, is a double who embodies the evil aspects of a character, and the passage tells us "Bertha represents the anger of all women in Victorian culture, ensnared in a patriarchal system that denied them rights and freedom." Choice A is not correct; the passage does not suggest that Bertha Mason serves as a pattern for Jane to follow, as an archetype does. C is not the credited answer; an anti-hero is a farcical take on the usual heroic characteristics. An antagonist is someone who acts against the main character; the passage does not suggest D as a reading. Eliminate E because a protagonist is the main character of a story.

CRITICAL READING

Questions 1–6 are based on the following passage.

The following passage is an excerpt from a book by novelist Gregor von Rezzori.

Skushno is a Russian word that is difficult to translate. It means more than dreary boredom: a spiritual void that sucks you in like a vague but intensely urgent longing.
Line When I was 13, at a phase that educators used to call the
5 awkward age, my parents were at their wits' end. We lived in the Bukovina, today an almost astronomically remote province in southeastern Europe. The story I am telling seems as distant—not only in space but also in time—as if I'd merely dreamed it. Yet it begins as a very
10 ordinary story.

I had been expelled by a *consilium abeundi*—an advisory board with authority to expel unworthy students—from the schools of the then Kingdom of Rumania, whose subjects we had become upon the collapse of the Austro-Hungarian
15 Empire after the first great war. An attempt to harmonize the imbalances in my character by means of strict discipline at a boarding school in Styria (my people still regarded Austria as our cultural homeland) nearly led to the same ignominious end, and only my pseudo-voluntary departure
20 from the institution in the nick of time prevented my final ostracism from the privileged ranks of those for whom the path to higher education was open. Again in the jargon of those assigned the responsible task of raising children to become "useful members of society," I was a "virtually
25 hopeless case." My parents, blind to how the contradictions within me had grown out of the highly charged indifference between their own natures, agreed with the schoolmasters; the mix of neurotic sensitivity and a tendency to violence, alert perception and inability to learn, tender need for sup-
30 port and lack of adjustability, would only develop into something criminal.

One of the trivial aphorisms my generation owes to Wilhelm Busch's *Pious Helene* is the homily "Once your reputation's done/You can live a life of fun." But this

35 optimistic notion results more from wishful thinking than from practical experience. In my case, had anyone asked me about my state of mind, I should have sighed and answered, "*Skushno!*" Even though rebellious thoughts occasionally surged within me, I dragged myself, or

40 rather I let myself be dragged, listlessly through my bleak existence in the snail's pace of days. Nor was I ever free of a sense of guilt, for my feeling guilty was not entirely foisted upon me by others; there were deep reasons I could not explain to myself; had I been able to do so, my life

45 would have been much easier.

1. It can be inferred from the passage that the author's parents were

   (A) frustrated by their son's inability to do well in school

   (B) oblivious to their son's poor academic performance

   (C) wealthy and insensitive to the needs of the poor

   (D) schoolmasters who believed in strict discipline

   (E) happy to live apart from their son

2. Lines 15–22 are used by the author to demonstrate that

   (A) the author was an unhappy and dangerous person

   (B) the schools that the author attended were too difficult

   (C) the tactics being used to make the author more stable were failing

   (D) the author was not well-accepted by his classmates

   (E) the author's academic career was nearing an end

3. The word "ignominious" in line 19 means

   (A) dangerous

   (B) pitiless

   (C) unappreciated

   (D) disgraceful

   (E) honorable

1. **A**   Use the lead word "parents" to guide you back to the passage. Where are the author's parents discussed? At the end of the second paragraph. In these lines, the passage says that his parents agreed with the schoolmasters that he was a "virtually hopeless case." The best paraphrase of this idea is A.

2. **C**   Carefully reread these lines. The passage states that the "attempt to harmonize the imbalances in [his] character by means of strict discipline at a boarding school in Styria... nearly led to the same ignominious end." The best paraphrase of this idea is C.

3. **D**   Cover up the word "ignominious" and put your own word in the blank. The word should mean something like "very unhappy" or "embarrassing." The choice that best fits this is D.

4. In line 21, the word "ostracism" most likely means

 (A) praise

 (B) abuse

 (C) appreciation

 (D) departure

 (E) banishment

5. The passage as a whole suggests that the author felt

 (A) happy because he was separated from his parents

 (B) upset because he was unable to maintain good friends

 (C) melancholy and unsettled in his environment

 (D) suicidal and desperate from living in Russia

 (E) hopeful because he would soon be finished with school

6. The passage indicates that the author regarded the aphorism mentioned in the last paragraph with

 (A) relief because it showed him that he would eventually feel better

 (B) disdain because the author found it unrealistic

 (C) contempt because he saw it working for others

 (D) bemusement because of his immunity to it

 (E) sorrow because his faith in it nearly killed him

4. **E**   Cover up the word "ostracism" and put your own word in the blank. The word should mean something like "thrown out" or "exiled." The choice that best fits this is E.

5. **C**   You know that the author is generally unhappy, so you can eliminate A and E. D is extreme, however, and should also be eliminated. Because the author never mentions his friends, you can eliminate B, and the best answer is C.

6. **B**   Reread the aphorism in context. Immediately following the aphorism, the author states that this "optimistic notion results more from wishful thinking than from practical experience." The best paraphrase of this idea is B.

Questions 1–8 are based on the following passages.

In Passage 1, the author presents his view of the early years of the silent film industry. In Passage 2, the author draws on her experiences as a mime to generalize about her art.

Passage 1

Talk to those people who first saw films when they were silent, and they will tell you that the experience was magic. The silent film had extraordinary powers to draw members
Line of an audience into the story, and an equally potent capacity
5 to make their imaginations work. It required the audience to become engaged—to supply voices and sound effects. The audience was the final, creative contributor to the process of making a film.

The finest films of the silent era depended on two elements
10 that we can seldom provide today—a large and receptive audience and a well-orchestrated score. For the audience, the fusion of picture and live music added up to more than the sum of the respective parts.

The one word that sums up the attitude of the silent film-
15 makers is enthusiasm, conveyed most strongly before formulas took shape and when there was more room for experimentation. This enthusiastic uncertainty often resulted in such accidental discoveries as new camera or editing techniques. Some films experimented with players; the 1915
20 film *Regeneration*, for example, by using real gangsters and streetwalkers, provided startling local color. Other films, particularly those of Thomas Ince, provided tragic endings as often as films by other companies supplied happy ones.

Unfortunately, the vast majority of silent films survive
25 today in inferior prints that no longer reflect the care that the original technicians put into them. The modern versions of silent films may appear jerky and flickery, but the vast picture palaces did not attract four to six thousand people per night by giving them eyestrain. A silent film
30 depends on its visuals; as soon as you degrade those, you lose elements that go far beyond the image on the surface. The acting in silents was often very subtle, very restrained, despite legends to the contrary.

Passage 2

Mime opens up a new world to the beholder, but it does
35 so insidiously, not by purposely injecting points of interest
in the manner of a tour guide. Audiences are not unlike
visitors to a foreign land who discover that the modes,
manners, and thoughts of its inhabitants are not meaningless oddities, but are sensible in context.

40 I remember once when an audience seemed perplexed at
what I was doing. At first, I tried to gain a more immedi-
ate response by using slight exaggerations. I soon realized
that these actions had nothing to do with the audience's
understanding of the character. What I had believed to
45 be a failure of the audience to respond in the manner I
expected was, in fact, only their concentration on what I
was doing; they were enjoying a gradual awakening—a
slow transference of their understanding from their own
time and place to one that appeared so unexpectedly
50 before their eyes. This was evidenced by their growing
response to succeeding numbers.

Mime is an elusive art, as its expression is entirely depen-
dent on the ability of the performer to imagine a character
and to re-create that character for each performance. As
55 a mime, I am a physical medium, the instrument upon
which the figures of my imagination play their dance of
life. The individuals in my audience also have responsi-
bilities—they must be alert collaborators. They cannot
sit back, mindlessly complacent, and wait to have their
60 emotions titillated by mesmeric music sounds or visual
rhythms or acrobatic feats, or by words that tell them what
to think. Mime is an art that, paradoxically, appeals both
to those who respond instinctively to entertainment and to
those whose appreciation is more analytical and complex.
65 Between these extremes lie those audiences conditioned
to resist any collaboration with what is played before
them; and these the mime must seduce despite themselves. There is only one way to attack those reluctant
minds—take them unaware! They will be delighted at an
70 unexpected pleasure.

1. Lines 11–13 of Passage 1 indicate that

   (A) music was the most important element of silent films

   (B) silent films rely on a combination of music and image in affecting an audience

   (C) the importance of music in silent film has been overestimated

   (D) live music compensated for the poor quality of silent film images

   (E) no film can succeed without a receptive audience

2. The "formulas" mentioned in line 16 of Passage 1 most probably refer to

   (A) movie theaters

   (B) use of real characters

   (C) standardized film techniques

   (D) the fusion of disparate elements

   (E) contemporary events

3. The author of Passage 1 uses the phrase "enthusiastic uncertainty" in line 17 to suggest that the filmmakers were

   (A) excited to be experimenting in an undefined area

   (B) delighted at the opportunity to study new acting formulas

   (C) optimistic in spite of the obstacles that faced them

   (D) eager to challenge existing conventions

   (E) eager to please but unsure of what the public wanted

1. **B**   Go back to the passage and read lines 11–13. Just before these lines, the passage says that a well-orchestrated score was important to silent films. On lines 11–13, the passage states that for the audience, the fusion of picture and live music was important. The choice that best paraphrases this idea is B.

2. **C**   Cover up the word "formulas" and put your own word in the blank. The word should mean something that does not allow experimentation. The best choice is C.

3. **A**   According to these lines in the passage, there was a great deal of experimentation that led to "such accidental discoveries as new camera or editing techniques." The choice that best paraphrases this idea is A.

4. The word "legends" in line 33 of Passage 1 most nearly means

    (A) fairy tales
    (B) symbolism
    (C) heroes
    (D) movie stars
    (E) misconceptions

5. The author of Passage 2 mentioned the incident in lines 40–47 in order to imply that

    (A) the audience's lack of response reflected their captivated interest in the performance
    (B) she was forced to resort to stereotypes in order to reach her audience
    (C) exaggeration is an essential part of mime
    (D) the audience had a good understanding of the subtlety of mime
    (E) vocalization is helpful in reaching certain audiences

6. Lines 40–47 indicate that the author of Passage 2 and the silent filmmakers of Passage 1 were similar because

    (A) neither used many props
    (B) both conveyed their message by using sophisticated technology
    (C) both learned through trial and error
    (D) both used visual effects and dialogue
    (E) both had a loyal following

4. **E**   Cover up the word "legends" and put your own word in the blank. The word should mean something like "false opinions" or "wrong ideas." The choice that fits this is E.

5. **A**   In lines 44–47, the author says "What I had believed to be a failure of the audience to respond in the manner I expected was, in fact, only their concentration on what I was doing . . . ." The choice that best paraphrases this idea is A.

6. **C**   Reread lines 40–47. If you're stuck, use POE. Because neither props nor sophisticated technology were ever mentioned, you can eliminate A and B. A loyal following is not mentioned in these lines either, so eliminate E. Choice D contradicts the point of the passage, because a mime does not use dialogue. Therefore, the answer must be C.

7. Lines 54–57 suggest that the author of Passage 2 feels that mimes

   (A) cannot control the way audiences interpret their characters

   (B) transform their bodies to portray their characters

   (C) have to resist outside attempts to define their acting style

   (D) should focus on important events in the lives of specific characters

   (E) know the limitations of performances that do not incorporate either music or speech

8. Passages 1 and 2 are similar in that both are mainly concerned with

   (A) the use of special effects

   (B) differences among dramatic styles

   (C) the visual aspects of performance

   (D) the suspension of disbelief in audiences

   (E) nostalgia for a bygone era

7. **B** Reread lines 54–57. These lines state that, "As a mime, I am a physical medium, the instrument upon which the figures of my imagination play their dance of life." The best paraphrase of this idea is B.

8. **C** POE is your best friend on this question. Special effects and suspension of disbelief are never mentioned, so eliminate A and D. Nostalgia is not part of Passage 2, so eliminate E. If you're stuck at this point, guess! The passage never actually discusses differences among styles, so the best answer is C.

BEYOND THE HIT PARADE

DON'T MEMORIZE THE DICTIONARY

Only a tiny percentage of all the words in the English language are ever used on the SAT. Generally speaking, the SAT tests the kinds of words that an educated adult—your English teacher, for example—would know without having to look them up. It tests the sorts of words that you encounter in your daily reading, from a novel in English class to the newspaper.

HOW TO MEMORIZE NEW WORDS

Here are three effective methods for learning new words.

1. **Flash Cards:** You can make your own flash cards out of 3 × 5 index cards. Write a word on one side and the definition on the other. Then quiz yourself on the words, or practice with a friend. You can carry a few cards around with you every day and work on them in spare moments, like when you're riding on the bus.

2. **The Image Approach:** The image approach involves letting each new word suggest a wild image to you, then using that image to help you remember the word. For example, the word *enfranchise* means "to give the right to vote." *Franchise* might suggest to you a McDonald's franchise. You could remember the new word by imagining people lined up to vote at a McDonald's. The weirder the image, the more likely you'll be to remember the word.

3. **Mnemonics:** Speaking of "the weirder, the better," another way to learn words is to use mnemonics. A mnemonic (the first "m" is silent) is a device or trick, such as a rhyme or a song, that helps you remember something. *In fourteen hundred ninety-two, Columbus sailed the ocean blue* is a mnemonic that helps you remember a date in history. The funnier or the stranger you make your mnemonic, the more likely you are to remember it. Write down your mnemonics (your flash cards are a great place for these).

Even if you are not able to think of a mnemonic for *every* Hit Parade word, sometimes you'll end up learning the word just by thinking about the definition long enough.

It will never hurt to add even more words to your study list, so we've gathered some additional words that have appeared on the SAT just in case you've already burned through the earlier lists.

abase
accolade
accretion
acumen
adapt
adroit
alacrity
alliance
altruism
amalgam
anachronistic
apathetic
arboreal
arcane
arrant
artless
ascertain
assimilate
astute
attenuated
augment
aural
autonomy
avarice
averse
awe
banal
barbarous
belie
belligerent
beneficial
bizarre
blandish
bolster

bombastic
brevity
cacophony
cadge
cajole
callous
calumniate
candid
canvass
captious
cartographer
castigate
cathartic
celerity
censure
chaos
chicanery
circumscribe
circumspect
competition
complement
conceive
conciliatory
conclusive
concord
concur
conjecture
consequence
conspicuous
contentious
contiguous
cosmopolitan
credible
cultivate

curative
dearth
debacle
debilitate
deft
defunct
demure
denounce
deride
derivative
derogatory
desuetude
detached
determined
devise
devoid
diffident
dirge
disaffected
discourse
disseminate
dissuade
distend
docile
duplicitous
effrontery
egress
eminent
empathy
endemic
enhance
enigma
epitome

equine
equivocal
eradicate
erratic
erudition
esoteric
esteem
euphemism
euphonious
exacerbate
exacting
exonerate
exorbitant
expedient
exscind
extent
extol
extraneous
extrapolate
exuberant
fallacy
fatuous
feign
felicitous
flaccid
flagrant
flippant
forbearance
forge
fragile
gaffe
generate
grandiose

halcyon
harsh
headstrong
heinous
hirsute
homily
humanity
hypodermic
ideal
idiosyncratic
ignominy
illumination
imbroglio
impetus
impractical
impugn
impulse
inane
incensed
inchoate
incipient
incoherent
incongruous
indict
innate
inoculate
inscrutable
insinuate
insular
intransigence
inundate
invocation
jaded
jejune
jettison

jibe
jocular
juxtapose
karma
lavish
lax
limn
limpid
litigious
loquacious
luculent
lugubrious
macerate
maculate
magnanimous
maleficent
mar
mediocrity
melancholy
mendacious
mercenary
modest
modicum
morose
multifarious
multiplicity
natty
nebulous
nefarious
nugatory
obeisance
obloquy
obsequious
obstinate
obtuse

officious
oligarchy
onerous
orthodox
outdated
palaver
palliative
panache
paradigm
parity
partisan
pedantic
pedestrian
pellucid
penchant
perfidy
pernicious
persist
perspective
perspicacious
philanthropic
pique
placid
portent
potentate
precocious
predominant
prescience
priggish
principle
profundity
proliferate
prolific
prospectus
proximity

pusillanimous
putrid
quell
quest
queue
quiescent
rapturous
raze
rebus
reciprocate
reclusive
rectitude
redolent
redouble
redundant
refractory
refute
relinquish
remiss
renounce
repudiate
resentment
rhetoric
rubric
rudimentary
salacious
sanctimonious
sardonic
scant
scintillating
scrupulous
servile
skeptical
solicitous
sporadic

squander
squelch
stand
standard
stentorian
stratify
strident
subjugate
substantiate
subterfuge
supercilious
supplant
sycophant
synergy
tangential
temperate
temporal
tenable
therapeutic
tractable
transparent
tumultuous
tyro
ubiquitous
unavailing

undermine
unscrupulous
upbraid
vacillate
validity
vapid
variegated
vaunt
veracity
verdant
vernacular
vex
vicarious
vigilant
vignette
vindictive
virago
vitality
vituperative
vivid
welter
wend
yeomanly
zenith

NOTES

NOTES

Expert advice from The Princeton Review

Increase your chances of getting into the college of your choice with **The Princeton Review!** We can help you ace your SATs, conquer your college applications, and find the best college for you.

Ace the SATs

Cracking the SAT, 2012 Edition
978-0-375-42829-6 • $21.99/$24.99 Can.

Cracking the SAT with DVD, 2012 Edition
978-0-375-42830-2 • $34.99/$40.99 Can.

11 Practice Tests for the SAT and PSAT, 2012 Edition
978-0-375-42837-1 • $22.99/$25.99 Can.

Crash Course for the SAT, 4th Edition
978-0-375-42831-9 • $9.99/$10.99 Can.

Math Workout for the SAT, 3rd Edition
978-0-375-42833-3 • $16.99/$18.99 Can.

Reading and Writing Workout for the SAT, 2nd Edition
978-0-375-42832-6 • $16.99/$18.99 Can.

Essential SAT Vocabulary (Flashcards)
978-0-375-42964-4 • $16.99/$21.99 Can.

Cracking the SAT Biology E/M Subject Test, 2011–2012 Edition
978-0-375-42810-4 • $19.99/$22.99 Can.

Cracking the SAT Chemistry Subject Test, 2011-2012 Edition
978-0-375-42814-2 • $19.99/$22.99 Can.

Cracking the SAT French Subject Test, 2011–2012 Edition
978-0-375-42815-9 • $19.99/$22.99 Can.

Cracking the SAT Literature Subject Test, 2011–2012 Edition
978-0-375-42811-1 • $19.99/$22.99 Can.

Cracking the SAT Math 1 & 2 Subject Tests, 2011–2012 Edition
978-0-375-42812-8 • $19.99/$22.99 Can.

Cracking the SAT Physics Subject Test, 2011–2012 Edition
978-0-375-42813-5 • $19.99/$22.99 Can.

Cracking the SAT Spanish Subject Test, 2011–2012 Edition
978-0-375-42817-3 • $19.99/$22.99 Can.

Cracking the SAT U.S. & World History Tests, 2011–2012 Edition
978-0-375-42816-6 • $19.99/$22.99 Can.

Find & Fund the Right School for You

The Best 376 Colleges, 2012 Edition
978-0-375-42839-5 • $22.99/$25.99 Can.

The Best Northeastern Colleges, 2011 Edition
978-0-375-42992-7 • $16.99/$18.99 Can.

College Essays that Made a Difference, 4th Edition
978-0-375-42785-5 • $13.99/$15.99 Can.

The Complete Book of Colleges, 2012 Edition
978-0-375-42739-8 • $26.99/$31.00 Can.

Paying for College Without Going Broke, 2011 Edition
978-0-375-42791-6 • $20.00/$23.00 Can.

Available everywhere books are sold and at PrincetonReviewBooks.com